P9-DHA-094

A Guide to *Biltmore Estate*

THE BILTMORE COMPANY

ASHEVILLE, NORTH CAROLINA

© 1997 The Biltmore Company

All rights reserved.

No part of this book may be reproduced or transmitted in any form or by any means, electronic or mechanical, including photocopying, recording, or by any information storage and retrieval system, without permission in writing from the publisher.

Biltmore Estate® is a registered trademark of The Biltmore Company.

Published by The Biltmore Company
One North Pack Square, Asheville, North Carolina 28801
800-543-2961 or 704-255-1700

Produced by
Rosemary G. Rennicke, Buckingham, Pennsylvania, and
Diane Maddex, Archetype Press, Inc., Washington, D.C.
Written by Rachel D. Carley and Rosemary G. Rennicke
Designed by Marc Alain Meadows and Robert L. Wiser, Archetype Press, Inc.
Project coordination at Biltmore Estate by Julia Weede and Jane Guignard Cox
Color photographs by Bill Alexander, Tim Barnwell, Richard Brown and Assoc., Cheryl Dalton, Terry Davis, Mike Smith, Sandy Stambaugh, James Valentine, and John Warner. Black-and-white photographs from Biltmore Estate archives.

Library of Congress Cataloging-in-Publication Data
Carley, Rachel.
A guide to Biltmore Estate / [written by Rachel Carley and Rosemary G. Rennicke].
    p.   cm.
ISBN 1-885378-00-9 (hardbound). — ISBN 1-885378-01-7 (paperbound)
1. Biltmore Estate (Asheville, N.C.) — Guidebooks.   2. Asheville (N.C.) — Buildings, structures, etc. — Guidebooks.   I. Title.
F264.A8C36   1994   94-11621
975.6'88—dc20   CIP

Front cover: Biltmore House at twilight. Copyright page: George Vanderbilt's bookplate. Back cover: The statue of Diana atop the Vista.

Printed in Italy

I NEVER KNEW MY GRANDFATHER, GEORGE VANDERBILT, but I cherish the memories of him that have been passed down through the family. I know, for example, that he loved to travel, and Biltmore is filled with the treasures he brought back from London, Paris, and Tokyo. I know, too, that he preferred horses to cars; you can see the beautiful park and woods where he used to go riding.

And most of all, I know he took special pride in sharing his home with others. From the first day Biltmore was opened, on Christmas Eve in 1895, it was often host to family and friends—everyone from famous artists to neighborhood children.

Guests are still a very important part of the Estate. Each one of you not only keeps alive the pleasure my grandfather took in entertaining but also maintains his ideal of a working estate that sustained itself and benefited the community. It is your support that allows Biltmore to remain self-sufficient and to be a leader in historic preservation through private enterprise.

I know my grandfather would certainly be pleased that so many people continue to visit his home—and perpetuate his dream. I hope, as you tour the Estate, that you enjoy yourself as thoroughly as the honored guests who have preceded you. And that you take home memories as precious as my own.

Welcome to Biltmore Estate.

Foreword

William A. V. Cecil

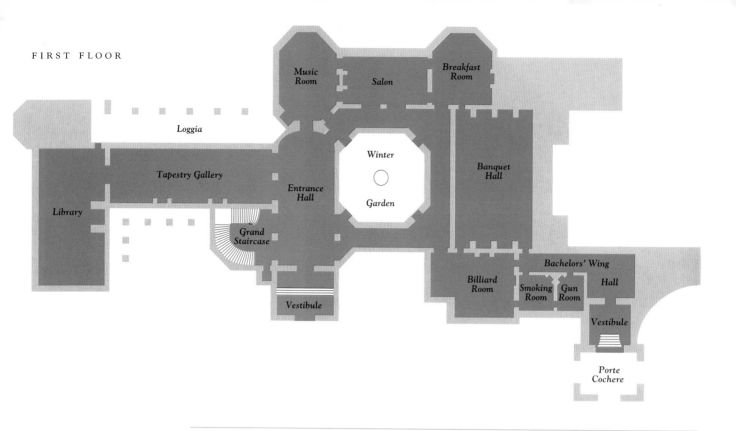

Contents

FOREWORD   WILLIAM A. V. CECIL   3

THE STORY OF BILTMORE   7

BILTMORE HOUSE   23
FIRST FLOOR   24
SECOND FLOOR   40
THIRD FLOOR   51
DOWNSTAIRS   61

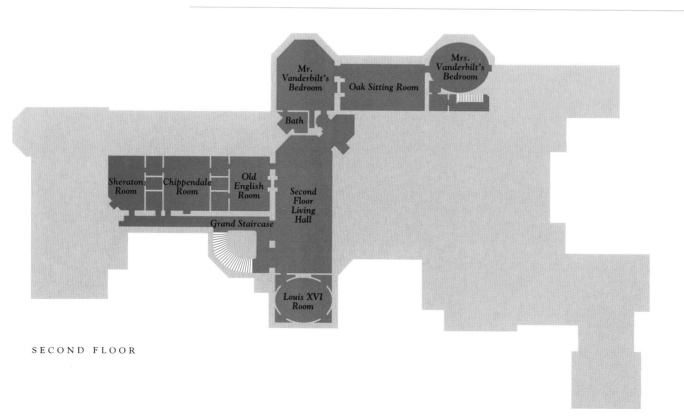

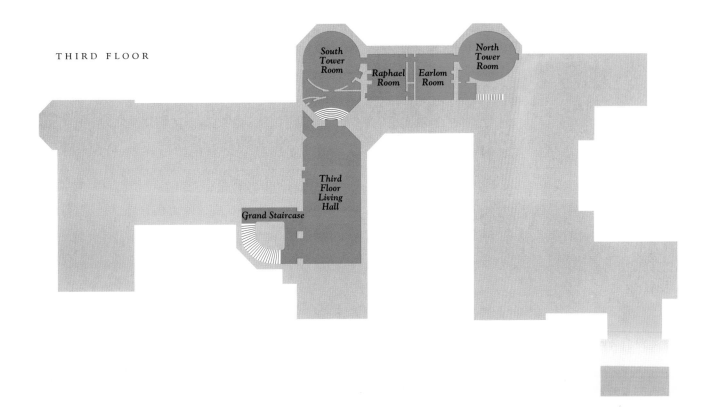

BACHELORS' WING 74

BEHIND THE SCENES 76

STABLE 80

BILTMORE GARDENS 83

BILTMORE ESTATE WINERY 99

BILTMORE HOUSE COLLECTIONS 108

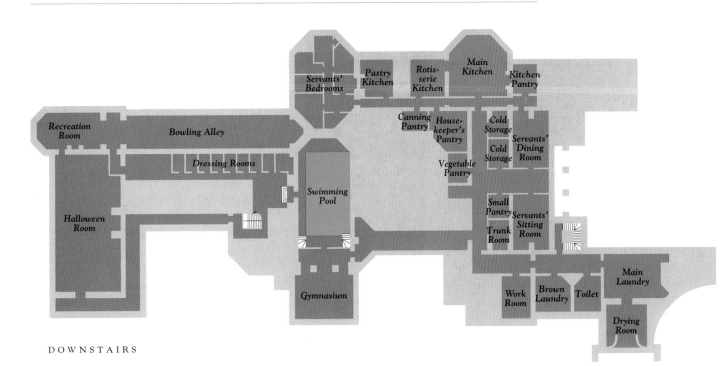

DOWNSTAIRS

The Story of Biltmore

Biltmore Estate is a testament to the uncompromising ideals of an exceptional man—George Washington Vanderbilt. What began as his vision of a country retreat became the largest private residence in America. And it stands to this day as a celebrated historic landmark. To visit Biltmore is to cross the threshold into a world of hospitality, beauty, and luxury that has remained unchanged for more than a century and is being preserved for many generations yet to come.

$\mathscr{W}$HEN GEORGE WASHINGTON VANDERBILT III WELCOMED family and friends to Biltmore Estate on Christmas Eve in 1895, his holiday celebration marked the formal opening of the most ambitious home ever conceived in America. For six years an army of artisans had labored to create a country estate that would rival the great manors of Europe and embody the finest in architecture, landscape planning, and interior design. The results were astounding.

Boasting four acres of floor space, the 250-room mansion featured 34 family and guest bedrooms, 43 bathrooms, 65 fireplaces, three kitchens, and an indoor swimming pool. It was appointed with a priceless collection of furnishings and artworks and equipped with every conceivable amenity, from elevators to refrigerators. The surrounding grounds were equally impressive, encompassing a 100,000-acre forest, a 250-acre wooded park, six pleasure gardens, and 30 miles of paved roadways.

The youngest in a family renowned for building palatial homes, 33-year-old George Vanderbilt had outdone them all.

A FAMILY LEGACY The Vanderbilts were not only one of the best-known families in America, they were also among the oldest: Jan Aertsen van der Bilt had emigrated to this country from Holland around 1650. Although his descendants prospered as farmers on Staten Island, New York, they lived modestly; it was only during the lifetime of Cornelius Vanderbilt (1794–1877) that the family name became synonymous with extraordinary wealth.

Legend holds that Cornelius changed the family fortune at age 16 with a $100 loan from his mother. Strong willed and self-educated, the budding entrepreneur

OPPOSITE: *George Vanderbilt, seen in a turn-of-the-century photograph on display in the Tapestry Gallery, was only 33 years old when he opened Biltmore.* ABOVE: *The Estate as it appeared in the late 1890s. It remains the largest private residence in America.*

ABOVE: *A patron of the arts and a collector of fine paintings, William Henry Vanderbilt commissioned* Going to the Opera—Family Portrait *from the American artist Seymour Guy in 1873. William Henry is seated at the left and is surrounded by his wife, their eight children, and other family members.*

launched a ferry service across New York Bay, which he eventually parlayed into a fleet of more than 100 steamboats that traveled as far as Central America and Europe. Some 50 years later the "Commodore," as he came to be called, earned his second fortune investing in railroads, the fabled New York Central among them.

Patriarch to a sizable family—including his wife of 53 years, Sophia, 13 children, 37 grandchildren, and 27 great-grandchildren—Cornelius established what became the Vanderbilt custom of luxurious residences. In the 1830s he raised an imposing three-story farmhouse with a grand colonnaded porch on Staten Island. He also began the tradition of philanthropy, contributing $1 million in 1873 to Central University, a Methodist school in Nashville; it was renamed Vanderbilt University.

Upon his death the Commodore left most of his $100 million estate—a sum that made him the wealthiest industrialist of his time—to his eldest son, William Henry (1821–85). Although his father had once considered him unsuited to business, William Henry took over the family empire and eventually doubled his assets. He, too, was generous toward worthy causes, funding the Metropolitan Opera in 1883 and endowing the

The Vanderbilt Family

The Vanderbilts are a large family descended in America from Jan Aertsen van der Bilt, who emigrated from Holland around 1650. The first family member to gain prominence was Cornelius, known as the "Commodore," who married Sophia Johnson in 1813 (both, top row, at left). Their eldest son was William Henry, who in 1841 married Maria Louisa Kissam (both, top row, at right). Their youngest child was George Washington, who wed Edith Stuyvesant Dresser in 1898 (both, at left). They had one child, Cornelia Stuyvesant (below left), who married John Cecil in 1924. The younger of their two sons is William Cecil, shown with his children and grandchildren (below right).

College of Physicians and Surgeons, now the Medical School of Columbia University.

The shrewd financier proved to be an equally astute collector, assembling more than 200 paintings. These were displayed in the 58-room mansion he built in 1881 at 640 Fifth Avenue—the largest and most splendid house in Manhattan. Outfitted with all the latest conveniences, such as telephones and refrigeration, the house was exquisitely decorated with European furniture, tapestries, stained-glass windows, and countless curios; it also had a glass-roofed stable courtyard so his beloved trotting horses could exercise without being exposed to the weather.

Only one of the eight children of William Henry and his wife, Maria Louisa (1821–96), was still living at home when the house was completed: the youngest, George, born in 1862. Quiet and intellectual, he had been greatly influenced by his father's cultural interests, starting his own collection of art and books at an early age; he even oversaw the design of his private quarters, including a library, in the new mansion. Significantly, George would inherit the house and its contents after his mother's death.

Unlike the rest of his family, however, George was little attracted to commerce and fashionable society. He instead preferred the world of learning and travel, having taken his first trip to Europe at age 10 and journeying to Europe, Asia, or Africa about once a year throughout his adult life. It was while traveling in the mountains of North Carolina that George first glimpsed his destiny.

ABOVE: *George Vanderbilt around 1874.* BELOW LEFT: *George's travel diary from 1880, when he sailed to Europe aboard the steamship* Brittanic *for a five-month tour of Italy, England, France, Switzerland, and Germany.* BELOW RIGHT: *Mr. Vanderbilt (seated, rear) cruised along the canals of Venice in the 1890s; the Doge's Palace and the Piazza San Marco are in the background.*

A VISION UNFOLDS Asheville was a popular health resort in the late 19th century, when train service brought tourists into the southern Appalachians to enjoy the mineral springs, fresh air, and pleasant climate. When George visited in 1888 with his mother, he was captivated by the rugged beauty of the rural region and found it the perfect setting for a new home.

Here it would be possible for George to fulfill his vision for an estate—one that would serve not only as a showcase for his cherished collections and a retreat for entertaining but also as a profitable, self-supporting business. He based his concept on the vast landed baronies he had seen in Europe, where country estates had endured for centuries, preserving both family and national heritage. He was also influenced by the Vanderbilt tradition of extravagant homes and by the 3,500-acre model farm, called Shelburne Farms, that his sister Lila had created in Vermont in 1886 with her husband, William Seward Webb.

ABOVE: *Biltmore Estate was the result of a collaboration among three talented men: Richard Morris Hunt (standing, second from left), George Washington Vanderbilt (standing, right), and Frederick Law Olmsted (sitting, center).*

As the first step toward his goal, George began purchasing parcels of land—which was both affordable and readily available in this area—eventually amassing 125,000 acres, including the 100,000-acre Pisgah Forest. He called the site "Biltmore"—from Bildt, the Dutch town where his ancestors originated, and "more," an old English word for open, rolling land. He then engaged two of the most distinguished designers of the 19th century: the architect Richard Morris Hunt (1828–95) and the landscape architect Frederick Law Olmsted (1822–1903).

George had known both men for several years; they collaborated on the family mausoleum on Staten Island that William Henry had commissioned in 1884. Hunt, the first American to study at the prestigious Ecole des Beaux-Arts in Paris, was the favorite society architect and became the unofficial family designer, creating Marble House and The Breakers in Newport, Rhode Island, and a mansion at 660 Fifth Avenue for George's brothers. He was also responsible for many important public works, such as the main facade of the Metropolitan Museum of Art in New York, the Yorktown Monument in Virginia, and the pedestal for the Statue of Liberty.

Olmsted, who was trained in engineering and agriculture and was known as the founding father of American landscape architecture, had designed scores of parks, most notably New York's Central Park, the U.S. Capitol grounds, and the campus of Stanford University in California. An early conservationist, he also consulted in 1864 on the preservation of Yosemite Valley, which became the site of America's first national park.

For these gifted professionals Biltmore represented the pinnacle of their long careers. Together with George they built not only an estate but also a close working relationship based on cooperation and respect.

BUILDING BEGINS Construction of Biltmore got under way in 1889; it was a massive undertaking that included a mansion, gardens, farms, and woodlands.

The centerpiece was a four-story stone house with a 780-foot-long front facade—a monument that would rival the surrounding mountains in grandeur. Hunt modeled the architecture on the richly ornamented style of the French Renaissance and adapted elements, such as the stair tower and the steeply pitched roof, from three famous early 16th-century châteaux in the Loire Valley: Blois, Chenonceau, and Chambord.

The interiors, too, were inspired by European estates, such as the English stately homes of Knole, Hatfield House, and Haddon Hall, which Hunt and his client had visited in 1889 while on a buying trip for furnishings. In fine Victorian fashion Biltmore was to be decorated with an eclectic assortment of European, American, and Oriental furniture and artworks in a range of period styles, along with custom-made pieces.

While Biltmore was to be a masterwork of design, it was also conceived as a marvel of modern technology. In addition to central heating, electricity, and a plumbing system that piped fresh water from a mountain reservoir several miles away, the House was equipped with fire alarms, mechanical refrigeration, and elevators.

Construction required a thousand artisans—from local laborers who earned 50 cents per day to acclaimed craftsmen, such as the Viennese sculptor Karl Bitter (1867–1915), a Hunt protégé hired to execute elaborate stone and wood carvings. Another noted contributor was the Spanish architect Rafael Guastavino (1842–1908), who had emigrated to America in the 1880s and quickly became known for the unique system for building tiled ceiling vaults that he had perfected.

BELOW: *Mr. Vanderbilt bought this photograph of the Château de Blois in 1889, during his trip to the Loire Valley with Hunt. The stair tower of the 16th-century French castle inspired the one at Biltmore, which spirals in the opposite direction.*

TOP LEFT: *Biltmore House was located on a bluff high above the confluence of the French Broad and Swannanoa rivers. In 1889 the site was occupied by farmland.* TOP RIGHT: *Building materials and work sheds covered the front court as construction proceeded. The rail line was installed to expedite delivery of supplies.* BOTTOM LEFT: *Scaffolding surrounds the stair tower and entrance door.* BOTTOM RIGHT: *About a thousand masons, carpenters, and other artisans worked on Biltmore House over the course of six years. Seen here are members of the construction crew in 1893.*

Among the countless tons of materials used were limestone hauled 600 miles from Indiana and marble imported from Italy. These and other supplies were delivered via a three-mile-long private rail spur laid between the depot in a neighboring village and the Estate. An on-site kiln produced some 32,000 bricks daily, and a woodworking factory processed oak and walnut for floors and paneling.

As the House was being built, work also progressed on the grounds. Because the tract had been overworked and the terrain was too "rough" for the extensive parkland George originally desired, Olmsted devised a more practical plan. He recommended installing a "small," 250-acre pleasure park and a series of gardens around the House, establishing farms along the fertile river bottoms, and replanting the rest of the property as commercial timber forest.

One of Olmsted's first projects was creating a nursery to supply the millions of plants needed for the grounds. In 1890 he hired as nursery superintendent Chauncey Beadle (1867–1950), a Canadian horticulturist who had been trained at Ontario Agricultural College and Cornell University. Beadle remained on the Estate for 60 years and guided Olmsted's plan to maturity. Gifford Pinchot (1865–1946) was engaged in 1891 to oversee renovation of the forest. A graduate of Yale University in 1889, Pinchot studied forestry at the Ecole Nationale Forestière in Nancy, France, and developed at Biltmore the first planned forestry program in America.

ESTATE LIFE After six years of construction Biltmore was opened on Christmas Eve 1895, when guests gathered to celebrate with a gaily trimmed tree, holiday feasts, and a coaching party. It was the first of many gala affairs on the Estate, which played host to such luminaries as the novelists Edith Wharton and Henry James and the society painter John Singer Sargent. Guests also came to relax and partake of a range of diversions, from tennis, archery, and croquet to picnicking, riding, and hunting; evenings brought musicales, parlor games, or perhaps a ball.

Guests could enjoy a range of entertainments, including hiking (above) and picnicking (above right) in the woodlands, playing croquet on the lawn of the Italian Garden (right), or going for a drive in a horse-drawn carriage (far right).

In addition to being used for entertaining, Biltmore was very much a home. It was here that George pursued his private interests in art, literature, and horticulture and also started a family. He married the American socialite Edith Stuyvesant Dresser (1873–1958) in June 1898 in Paris, and the couple came to live at the Estate that fall after honeymooning in Europe. Their only child, Cornelia (1900–76), was born and grew up at Biltmore.

The Vanderbilts were attended by an 80-person staff, including domestic servants and stable hands, and were known as kind and generous employers. Besides paying good wages and providing comfortable living quarters, they held a Christmas party for the staff each year as a special measure of thanks, decorating an enormous tree with gifts for employees' children.

As the new century progressed, George was able to realize his dream of a productive estate. The farms yielded fruits, vegetables, grain crops, meat and dairy products, and honey from 41 beehives. The forest produced some 3,000 cords of firewood annually, which was sold along with lumber processed at Biltmore's own mill. And the 300-

FAR LEFT: *Estate employees lined the Approach Road in October 1898 to welcome newlyweds George and Edith to Biltmore.* LEFT: *George proudly shows off the infant Cornelia, born in 1900.* BELOW LEFT: *Cornelia hosts her cousin John Brown at a tea party around 1905.* BELOW: *Edith and Cornelia lead a parade of carriages through the streets of Biltmore Village in 1906.*

ABOVE: *The Vanderbilts started two schools in the early 1900s: Biltmore Industries (left), which taught handcraft skills, and the School for Domestic Science (right), which taught housekeeping.*

acre nursery, complete with greenhouses, cold frames, and seed beds, offered for sale about five million plants—one of the most complete stocks in the country until it was destroyed by flood in 1916.

Both George and Edith were also committed to helping others. In 1889 George had purchased the little nearby town of Best, which he renamed Biltmore Village and enlarged between 1896 and 1902 to include a school, a hospital, a church, shops, and cottages outfitted with plumbing and central heating. He introduced innovative farming techniques to the rural region and championed the founding of the Biltmore Forest School in 1898—the first institute for scientific forestry in America.

In 1901 the Vanderbilts started Biltmore Industries, an apprenticeship program to teach such traditional handcrafts as woodworking and weaving. Students often made reproductions of Biltmore furnishings and sold their work to earn a living. Two years later Edith set up the School for Domestic Science, which trained young women in housekeeping skills.

YEARS OF CHANGE While the Vanderbilts owned several other residences, George was actively involved with the operation of Biltmore until his unexpected death in March 1914, following an emergency appendectomy in Washington, D.C. After his

burial in the family mausoleum, Edith returned to the Estate and resumed her work in the community, becoming the first woman president of the state agricultural society, helping build a new hospital, and advocating literacy programs.

After a time, however, she found managing such a large property to be overwhelming and began consolidating her interests. Honoring her husband's wish to preserve Pisgah Forest for the public, she deeded nearly 87,000 acres to the federal government in 1915 to create the nucleus of Pisgah National Forest. She sold Biltmore Industries in 1917 and Biltmore Village in 1921; by the late 1920s, the Estate had been reduced in size to about 11,000 acres (it is currently 8,000 acres).

In 1925 Edith married Senator Peter G. Gerry and moved to his home state of Rhode Island and to Washington, D.C. Cornelia continued to live at Biltmore; she had been married the year before at All Souls Church in Biltmore Village to the Honorable John Francis Amherst Cecil (1890–1954), a descendant of William Cecil (1520–98), Lord Burghley, who was Lord High Treasurer to Queen Elizabeth I. Their two sons, George Henry Vanderbilt Cecil and William Amherst Vanderbilt Cecil, were born on the Estate in 1925 and 1928, respectively.

Biltmore continued to serve the region, just as it had in George's day. Acting on a request by the city of Asheville, which hoped to revitalize the Depression-era

ABOVE LEFT: *All Souls Church under construction in Biltmore Village.* ABOVE RIGHT: *The first woman president of the North Carolina Agricultural Society, Edith takes the wheel of a tractor as Cornelia looks on.* BELOW: *Cornelia and John Cecil with their first child, George. Both of their sons were born at Biltmore Estate.*

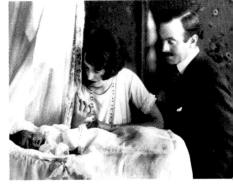

economy with tourism, the Cecils opened the Estate to the public for the first time in March 1930. During World War II, when the capital was under threat of air attack, priceless artworks from the National Gallery of Art were sent to the House for safe-keeping. And the Biltmore dairy grew into a thriving enterprise that provided both employment and top-quality products.

BILTMORE TODAY In 1960 William Cecil left a banking career in New York City and Washington, D.C., to join his brother in managing Biltmore, which they inherited under the terms of a trust. His goal was not only to return the historic site to its turn-of-the-century splendor but also to perpetuate his grandfather's ideal of self-sufficiency.

Under Mr. Cecil's stewardship, more than 90 rooms, with some 70,000 original objects, have been opened to the public. The ongoing preservation program he instituted makes it possible to experience the Estate as it was during the Vanderbilts' residence. Mrs. Vanderbilt's Bedroom, for instance, was restored in 1990 using exact

BELOW: *Biltmore's textile conservators repair one of the eight 16th-century tapestries collected by Mr. Vanderbilt.*

duplicates of the original French fabrics—woven on the same looms used in the 1890s. In the Library the 2,000-square-foot ceiling painting was removed, restored, and reinstalled. One of the most complex projects undertaken is the cleaning and repair of the eight 16th-century Flemish tapestries in the collection, now being carried out by Biltmore's own expert staff of textile conservators.

Mr. Cecil also brought changes to Biltmore to keep it a vital, living landmark. After the dairy, under the leadership of George Cecil, became a separate business in 1979, the dairy barn was remodeled for use as a winery, which has become the most visited wine-making facility in America. Angus and Limousin beef cattle have been introduced in the farm operation, and a breeding program has produced several champions. And each winter Candlelight Christmas Evenings in the House, which is decorated with nearly 40 trees, rekindle the festive spirit of a Victorian holiday.

In keeping with George Vanderbilt's vision, Biltmore, which was named a National Historic Landmark in 1963, is entirely self-sustaining, receiving neither government subsidies nor private grants. Its operations and preservation efforts are supported by a variety of ventures, including selective timber harvesting and The Biltmore Estate Collection, a line of finely crafted reproduction furnishings available for sale, as well as by guest admissions. The Estate, with a staff of 650, also contributes to the community as one of the region's largest employers.

ABOVE: The Loggia outside the Library glows as the sun sets over the Deerpark.

Perhaps most important, Biltmore today maintains the tradition of hospitality engendered by its founder, welcoming more than 750,000 guests each year. Just as it has since 1895, the Estate continues to attract visitors to its celebrated house and gardens and to inspire in all who see it the same awe and wonder that it elicited upon first opening its doors.

Biltmore House

No residence in America brings the glorious Gilded Age more vividly to life than Biltmore House. More than 90 rooms, faithfully preserved and filled with thousands of original furnishings, suggest that the Vanderbilts are still at home. From the opulent living quarters enjoyed by family and friends to the "downstairs" domain of the domestic staff, the House presents a detailed portrait of a great 19th-century country estate.

*O*N THE MAIN FLOOR OF BILTMORE ARE THE PUBLIC rooms in which the Vanderbilts lived as a family and entertained their guests. Arranged around a light-filled garden court are an entry hall, a game room, and several dining and sitting areas; set off by itself is an expansive library, a quiet retreat for study or solitude. The decor throughout is lavish, with marble and mahogany, silk and crystal, silver and gilt expressing the Victorian taste for finery.

ENTRANCE HALL With its soaring limestone arches and polished marble floor, the Entrance Hall serves as an impressive introduction to Biltmore House. The focal point is a massive oak table designed by Richard Morris Hunt, which displays a group of bronzes by Antoine-Louis Barye (1796–1875), the renowned French artist. Inspired by the 16th-century Italian epic poem *Orlando Furioso*, the center sculpture portrays the hero, Roger, rescuing his love, Angelique, on a mythical creature called the Hippogriff. The flanking candelabra are modeled with figures of the Roman goddesses Juno, Minerva, and Venus.

WINTER GARDEN Glass-roofed garden rooms were considered quite stylish in the Victorian era, providing a place to relax or entertain amid an indoor "jungle" of exotic plants. Also fashionable, especially for garden use, was rattan and bamboo furniture, such as this suite bought by Mr. Vanderbilt in France. Complementing the garden setting is a marble fountain crowned with a bronze statue of a boy with two geese—the work of Karl Bitter, a Viennese sculptor who emigrated to America in 1889.

The adjoining corridor features tiled ceiling vaults designed by the Spanish architect Rafael Guastavino. On the walls are plaster copies of sections of the frieze on the Parthenon in Athens; they were crafted in the 1800s by Eugene Arrondelle of the Louvre in Paris.

ABOVE: *Preserved in the pages of the Nonsense Book, a type of scrapbook for Biltmore's guests, is a sketch drawn in 1902 of Karl Bitter's bronze figures.* RIGHT: *Cornelia Vanderbilt and John Cecil held their wedding breakfast by the fountain in 1924.* OPPOSITE: *At Christmastime the palms, ficus, and other tropical plants in the Winter Garden are joined by colorful poinsettias.*

BILLIARD ROOM Part of a series of rooms known as the Bachelors' Wing, the Billiard Room provided a separate retreat for Mr. Vanderbilt and his male guests. (Hidden doors on either side of the fireplace lead to other rooms in the wing.) Here they could enjoy each other's company and indulge in billiards, played on the carom table (with no pockets), or pool, played on the pool table (with six pockets). Both games became so popular in the 1800s that special rooms like this began to appear at country estates — supposedly to protect the rest of the household from the noisy pastime.

The nucleus of the male domain, the Billiard Room resembles the exclusive gentlemen's social clubs in vogue among Victorians — with somber oak paneling, an ornamental plaster ceiling, and a herringbone-patterned floor covered with deep-hued Oriental carpets. Equally masculine are the leather settees and armchairs made in London in 1895; the pieces are reproductions of 17th-century furniture from Knole, an English estate that Mr. Vanderbilt and Hunt visited in 1889.

Displayed around the room are examples from Mr. Vanderbilt's print collection. Many of the works are based on paintings by the British artists Sir Joshua Reynolds (1723–92), George Stubbs (1724–1806), and Sir Edwin Landseer (1802–73). Above the sofa is the painting *Rosita* by Ignacio Zuloaga y Zaboleta (1870–1945), a highly regarded Spanish genre and portrait painter.

OPPOSITE: *Illuminated by wrought-iron light fixtures made especially for the room, the American oak game tables are each topped with three slabs of slate weighing about 900 pounds. The balls are ivory, and many of the 24 cue sticks, stored in their original oak stands, are inlaid with ivory and mother-of-pearl.*

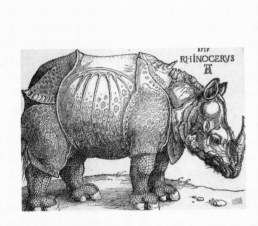

Prints

Mr. Vanderbilt was an avid collector of prints, acquiring about 1,600 etchings, woodcuts, aquatints, photogravures, and other printed works throughout his life. Examples from the collection, which includes sporting, architecture, landscape, still-life, and portrait prints, are (clockwise from above left) Rhinocerus, *a 1515 woodcut by Albrecht Dürer; a likeness of Cardinal Richelieu engraved in 1657 by Robert Nanteuil; and* Chartres: Street Scene and Cathedral, *an 1882 etching by Axel Haig.*

INSET, RIGHT: *Karl Bitter is shown with the oak panels he carved between 1893 and 1895 for the organ loft. The figures (below) depict characters from Tannhäuser, an opera by the 19th-century German composer Richard Wagner.* OPPOSITE: *Although massive in proportion, the Banquet Hall has perfect acoustics: two people sitting at opposite ends of the dining table could converse without having to raise their voices.*

BANQUET HALL As imposing as a great hall in a medieval castle, the Banquet Hall is the largest room in the House, measuring 72 feet long by 42 feet wide with a 70-foot-high barrel-vaulted ceiling. It was in this baronial space that the Vanderbilts entertained formally, hosted birthday parties for Cornelia, and held their annual Christmas festivities—a tradition that continues to this day.

Because of the room's vast dimensions, Hunt designed special furniture for it, including two gilt-trimmed throne chairs and an oak dining table that can accommodate 64 people. The architect also created a suitable setting for the five Flemish tapestries that Mr. Vanderbilt is thought to have purchased in Paris in 1887. These intricate textiles, woven of silk, wool, and metallic thread between 1546 and 1553, are part of an original set of seven portraying the story from Roman mythology of Venus (goddess of love); her paramour, Mars (god of war); and her jealous husband, Vulcan (god of fire).

The triple fireplace, which is flanked with armor dating from the 1400s to 1800s, features on its overmantel a bas-relief panel entitled *The Return from the Chase.* It was carved by Bitter, who was also responsible for the oak mural on the organ gallery. Although organs were common features in halls, an instrument was never installed here and the back rank of pipes is not operational. Below are arched niches holding a collection of 18th- and 19th-century brass and copper vessels from Holland, France, and Spain.

The pennants hanging in the room include the Biltmore Estate service flag, commemorating staff members who fought in World War I, and replicas of flags from the American Revolution and the 13 original colonies. Those hanging above the fireplace represent countries in power when Christopher Columbus sailed to North America; the 400th anniversary of his second voyage was celebrated in 1893 by the World's Columbian Exposition in Chicago, which Mr. Vanderbilt visited.

ABOVE: *Each of the hundreds of pieces in the family table service bears a monogram; this tureen is marked with "CSV" for Cornelia Stuyvesant Vanderbilt.* OPPOSITE: *As part of the complete restoration of the Breakfast Room in 1993, the seating pieces were reupholstered and the draperies were replaced using 350 yards of silk cut velvet matched to the original pattern. The fabric was woven by Tassinari & Chatel of Lyons, France— the same textile firm that filled Mr. Vanderbilt's order in the 1890s.*

BREAKFAST ROOM Designed on a more intimate scale than the Banquet Hall, this room was intended for less formal dining and was used for all three meals—not just breakfast. Nevertheless, the room is elegant, with Italian marble wainscoting and door trim, a tooled-leather wall covering, and a fireplace surround of Wedgwood jasperware tiles. The ornate plasterwork ceiling is highlighted with a gold-tinted glaze and features heavy pendants that terminate in tiny acorns—one of the symbols in the Vanderbilt family crest.

No finery was spared in setting the table, which was spread with embroidered damask linens from Paris. Seated on gilt-legged chairs with cut-velvet upholstery, diners were served their meals on gold-trimmed porcelain dinnerware made by Minton and Spode, two noted Staffordshire potteries. And they drank from crystal glasses—etched with the Vanderbilt monogram—produced by Baccarat of France and Thomas Webb and Sons of England.

Among the family portraits in this room are likenesses of Mr. Vanderbilt's father, William Henry, hanging over the display case, and of his mother, Maria Louisa, seen to the right of the fireplace. There are two paintings of his grandfather, Cornelius: the circa 1839 portrait to the left of the fireplace shows him as a young man (appropriately, for a mariner, holding a spyglass) and the circa 1876 portrait above the door to the Banquet Hall depicts him as a successful businessman.

OPPOSITE: *The Salon boasts one of the many interesting ceiling treatments used throughout the House. It is draped with wool brocade* *tenting, a feature perhaps inspired by the Victorian passion for exotic Oriental and Moorish decorating styles.*

SALON Just as the men of the household adjourned to the Billiard Room, women would retire to the Salon for conversation or reading; they might even step out on the adjoining balcony to take some air and view the landscape. The decor features graceful French furniture, including 19th-century Louis XV-style seating pieces with their original tapestry-weave upholstery and a folding screen with petit-point panels. The room is also a showcase for prints by Albrecht Dürer (1471–1528), the noted artist of the Northern Renaissance, and prints of châteaux in the Loire Valley.

At each end of the room are hangings made for Cardinal Richelieu, the 17th-century French statesman; such furnishings were used at the time as decoration behind the chairs of high-ranking officials. Stitched with embroidery and metal-thread couching, the velvet textiles depict his armorial bearings, hat, and Latin motto, *Semper Idem*, meaning "always the same."

Reflecting Mr. Vanderbilt's interest in the Napoleonic era is the Empire walnut game table and ivory chess pieces that had been owned and used by Napoleon Bonaparte during his exile on St. Helena island between 1815 and 1821. After the deposed emperor's death, his heart was placed in a silver urn on the table before being put into his coffin.

Games

The Victorian era was the golden age of games; for the first time most people had enough leisure to enjoy such indoor entertainment, thus causing a boom in board, card, table, and parlor games. At Biltmore family and guests had a choice of pleasant pastimes, from cribbage to checkers. Card games, such as whist and euchre, were played upstairs and downstairs with gaily decorated decks (top). Chess was played on a 19th-century game table with ivory pieces (above left) originally owned by Napoleon Bonaparte. Gentlemen gamblers used poker chips and an American-made walnut roulette wheel (above right). Mah-jongg was a popular Chinese game using tiles, and Biltmore had a set (right) from Hong Kong.

MUSIC ROOM Plans for Biltmore indicate that a music room was intended for this location, although it was never finished; what had been an empty space with bare brick walls was renovated and opened in 1976. The room is decorated to reflect the French Renaissance style and includes such period touches as linen-fold wall paneling, which was carved of red oak harvested from Biltmore's forest, and polychrome painting on the boxed beams.

The room was also conceived to display several treasures. The fireplace mantel—which was found stored below the stables—had been designed by Hunt and carved with Albrecht Dürer's initials and life dates. Above it hangs a 19th-century printing of the woodcut known as the *Triumphal*

Arch, which Holy Roman Emperor Maximilian I (1459–1519) commissioned from Dürer around 1515. Measuring about 10 feet tall by 10 feet wide, the work depicts military and political events, references to the emperor's prowess as a hunter and linguist, and a family tree peopled with mythological characters.

On the shelves beside the print is a rare collection of 12 apostle figures and 12 candlesticks. Based on statuary in the Basilica of St. John Lateran in Rome, the gilt-trimmed porcelain sculptures are the work of Johann Joachim Kändler (1706–75), who was master modeler at the Meissen factory near Dresden. The pieces may have come from several different sets made between 1735 and 1741 for Empresses Amalia and Maria Theresa of the Austrian Hapsburgs.

INSET, ABOVE: *The figure of St. Matthew is part of a set portraying the 12 apostles that was produced by the Meissen porcelain factory in the mid-1700s. The base is marked with the Austrian imperial crest; the Biltmore sculptures are the only known collection bearing this eagle insignia.* BELOW: *A detail from the monumental Triumphal Arch, designed by Albrecht Dürer.*

Comprising 192 separately printed blocks, the work arrived at Biltmore just before Christmas 1895, shipped by train in three boxes.

OPPOSITE: *Unfinished during Mr. Vanderbilt's lifetime, the Music Room is today outfitted with a Steinway piano—played by Van Cliburn during his visit to the Estate in 1961—and an elaborately carved and gilded 18th-century music stand.*

TAPESTRY GALLERY Opening off the Entrance Hall, this 90-foot-long room served as a sitting area and, it is believed, a ballroom. (The English sofas and club chairs are fitted with casters and would have been easy to clear out of the way.) The space was also intended as an exhibition gallery for three silk-and-wool tapestries woven in Brussels around 1530. Part of an original set of seven known as *The Triumph of the Seven Virtues*, the pieces are distinguished by richly detailed pictorial designs that personify Prudence, Faith, and Charity and incorporate biblical, mythological, and historical images.

Other notable furnishings include three 19th-century Persian rugs—examples of the several hundred Eastern carpets Mr. Vanderbilt acquired on his trips to Europe. Indeed, a receipt from 1889 reveals that he bought 300 carpets from a London dealer at one time. Not all the furniture, however, came from abroad. The two gateleg tables with spiral-twist legs were produced by Biltmore Industries, the handcraft program founded by the Vanderbilts in 1901.

Three family portraits hang on the paneled wall to the Library. Over the door is the likeness of George Vanderbilt, painted in 1895, and to the left is that of his mother, Maria Louisa Kissam Vanderbilt, painted around 1888. Both are the work of John Singer Sargent (1856–1925), one of the most celebrated society portraitists of his time. On the right is Edith Vanderbilt by Giovanni Boldini (1842–1931), an Italian artist who enjoyed an international reputation at the turn of the century. On the opposite wall is another likeness of Edith Vanderbilt; entitled *Ivory and Gold*, it was done in 1902 by James Abbott McNeill Whistler (1834–1903), the famous American expatriate painter.

LEFT: *Providing a colorful setting for three 16th-century Flemish tapestries are stenciled ceiling beams and painted limestone fireplace hoods modeled after those in the Château de Pierrefonds near Compiègne, France.*
ABOVE: *A fearsome serpent (this is one of its three heads) forms part of the complex design in a tapestry depicting the virtue of Prudence.*

LIBRARY Of all the rooms in Biltmore House, the Library best reflects Mr. Vanderbilt's intellect and personality. An avid reader and book lover from childhood—George had already started acquiring books by age 11—he amassed a collection of more than 23,000 volumes in eight languages, about 10,000 of which are housed in the Library's walnut stacks. His interests were wide-ranging, as evidenced by books on everything from architecture to agriculture.

While the Library served as a personal retreat, Mr. Vanderbilt also enjoyed sharing it. A passage leading from behind the fireplace to the guest quarters provided direct access to the room, making it easy for visitors to select a volume for bedtime reading. (Even so, Henry James, the noted American author who visited Biltmore in 1905, complained that his bedroom was at least half a mile away from the "mile-long library.")

Among the striking features of the room is a dramatic ceiling painting—*The Chariot of Aurora*, by the Venetian artist Giovanni Antonio Pellegrini (1675–1741). Originally located in the ballroom of the Pisani Palace in Venice, the work comprises 13 separate canvases and measures about 64 feet long by 32 feet wide.

Equally impressive are the black marble fireplace surround and the walnut overmantel, both carved by Bitter. The figures of Demeter, goddess of the earth (with legs crossed), and Hestia, goddess of the hearth, flank the 17th-century French tapestry.

OPPOSITE: *Stocked with books dating as early as 1561, the Library was a source of both recreation and information for its scholarly owner, who employed a librarian to catalog his 23,000-volume collection.*

ABOVE LEFT: *Making the room appear open to the sky, the ceiling painting represents dawn. It is one of the most important canvases by Pellegrini extant, as many of his works were destroyed in the world wars.*

ABOVE RIGHT: *In this circa 1898 photograph, Cedric, one of the family's St. Bernards, rests beside an ornate reading table designed by Hunt.*

WHEREAS THE FIRST FLOOR HOUSED THE COMMUNAL rooms, the second story was home to the Vanderbilts' private quarters, along with a series of guest suites. The floor is organized around a central sitting area where men and women could socialize without invading the privacy of a bedroom—an essential arrangement in an age of modesty and decorum. This and two other upper floors could be reached by either a staircase or an Otis elevator, which traveled 100 feet per minute and was the first passenger elevator in Asheville.

LOUIS XVI ROOM One of 32 guest rooms at Biltmore—needed to accommodate the Vanderbilts' large house parties—the Louis XVI Room exemplifies the rage for French decorating styles in the late 19th century. A broad array of furniture forms and ornamental motifs that had been fashionable in France between the 1500s and 1700s was rediscovered and reproduced on both sides of the Atlantic from the 1860s to 1900.

Perhaps the most popular of the revivals was the Louis XVI style, named for the king under whose reign it originated in the mid-18th century. The clean, classical style, which was influenced by the excavations at Pompeii in 1748, is characterized by straight lines, gilded and carved decoration, and designs derived from ancient Greek and Roman art.

Reflecting this style are the chaise, settee, side chairs, and center table—all 19th-century French pieces with slender, reeded legs and delicate swag or scroll motifs. The inlaid-kingwood bed, from the early 1900s, and the kidney-shaped rosewood parquetry table, from the 1800s, feature brass mounts. Red damask upholstery and wall covering, as well as the lightly patterned Aubusson carpets, contribute to the refined look of the oval room.

ABOVE LEFT: *The 102-step Grand Staircase stretches to the fourth floor. Running through its center is a 1,700-pound wrought-iron chandelier illuminated by 72 electric bulbs—thought to be the world's largest such fixture suspended from a single point.*

ABOVE RIGHT: *This desk set is made of faience, or tin-glazed earthenware, and was probably produced at the noted 18th-century French pottery of La veuve Perrin in Marseilles. It was used to hold an inkwell, a pounce pot, quills, and wax wafers for sealing letters.*

OPPOSITE: *The Louis XVI Room is one of several bedrooms designed in an oval, a shape that was in vogue for interiors in 18th-century France. The shape and size of this room seem to dwarf the bed, which is, in fact, a six-foot-long double bed.*

SECOND FLOOR LIVING HALL A Victorian lady or gentleman concerned with propriety would never consider entertaining a member of the opposite sex in a bedroom. Hence the Living Hall—a common area where occupants of the second-floor guest rooms, along with family members, could mingle informally before meals or spend a lazy afternoon reading or chatting. Upholstered furniture in intimate groupings invited conversation, while a handsome Louis XIV-style desk offered a perfect place for letter writing.

Today the room serves as a gallery for several important paintings. In prominent positions on the north wall are full-length portraits of the two architects who helped translate Mr. Vanderbilt's vision for the Estate into reality. On the right is Frederick Law Olmsted; the landscape designer is fittingly shown in a woodland setting beside a blossoming rhododendron. On the left is Richard Morris Hunt, who is posed in front of the outside stair tower (although

the weather was so chilly when the portrait was done that he actually stood indoors by a fireplace). Both were painted by Sargent, who came to Biltmore in May 1895 to capture these men on canvas. Between them hangs *The Waltz* by Anders Zorn (1860–1920), the respected Swedish artist; Mr. Vanderbilt purchased the painting in 1893 at the World's Columbian Exposition in Chicago, where it was on exhibit.

Family portraits include a likeness of Cornelia Vanderbilt Cecil, painted in the 1920s by the Russian artist Nikol Schattenstein (1877–1955). The group portrait at the east end is of the William Cecil family, painted by the prominent New York artist and native Ashevillian Stone Roberts (1951–).

At the opposite end hangs *Going to the Opera—Family Portrait*, depicting the William Henry Vanderbilt family, by the American painter Seymour Guy (1824–75); 11-year-old George is seated at the table.

OPPOSITE: *The two tones of brown on the walls of the Living Hall are affectionately known as "coffee and tea." This color scheme is found throughout the House to indicate areas for family and guests; rooms for staff, in turn, are painted green. Such color coding was traditionally used in English country houses to help guests find their way through the oft-confusing mazes of rooms.*

Clocks

Among the most intricate and varied objects at Biltmore are the clocks—from the tall-case clock in the Entrance Hall to the massive tower clock on the Stable to the mirror-mounted cartel clock in the Louis XVI Room. The 25 timepieces in the collection range from the mid-17th century to the early 20th century and were made primarily in England and France. Shown here are a circa 1780 arch-top bracket clock (far left) by Coward and Company, a gilt-and-bronze statue clock (top left) with works by Japy Frères from around 1870, and an inverted basket-top bracket clock (bottom left) made by Edmund Card in the late 1600s.

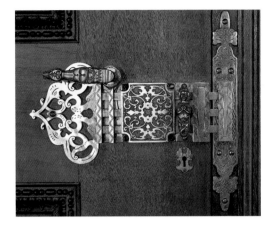

TOP LEFT: *No detail in the bedroom was overlooked: the elaborate brass door latch was hand cast with floral and figural elements specifically for the room.* TOP RIGHT: *Mr. Vanderbilt's bathroom, plumbed with hot and cold running water, features a paw-footed tub.* RIGHT: *The bronze bust of Mr. Vanderbilt was created by the Scottish artist Mary Grant in 1889; it is displayed in the Library.* OPPOSITE: *Befitting the head of the household is this dignified room, with deep ceiling moldings and a gold-glazed wall covering. While the bed is from 17th-century Portugal, the large turned-leg table was designed by Hunt and manufactured around 1894 by Baumgarten & Co., a New York City decorating firm.*

MR. VANDERBILT'S BEDROOM The owner of Biltmore was a man accustomed to the best, and he settled for nothing less in siting and furnishing his bedroom. It is located in the southwest corner of the House, where he could enjoy a commanding view of his property— from the wooded Deerpark below to Mount Pisgah, 17 miles in the distance. And the room is filled with heavily carved and turned walnut pieces, including a dressing table, a chaise, and chairs, that were designed by Hunt and inspired by styles of the Renaissance.

Mr. Vanderbilt also surrounded himself with the art objects he loved, such as fine engravings by 16th- and 17th-century artists from Germany and Holland and bronze sculptures from 19th-century France.

Through the door beside the bed is Mr. Vanderbilt's bath—another example of his insistence on the finest appointments. The full-length mirror reflects his marble bathtub, which was a luxury at the time. Even though indoor plumbing was found in affluent homes as early as the 1830s, fully equipped bathrooms—with a toilet, sink, and bath or shower—were still far from common in the 1890s. Rarer still was hot water available instantly at the turn of the tap, which was provided by two coke-fired hot-water heaters in the sub-basement.

OPPOSITE: *The private, family equivalent of the Living Hall, this richly appointed room served as a sitting area for the Vanderbilts. It is filled with treasures, including Eastern carpets, Oriental porcelains, and French bronzes.*

OAK SITTING ROOM Connecting Mr. and Mrs. Vanderbilt's private quarters, this well-appointed room was used as a private sitting area for the couple. The architectural detailing throughout is extremely ornate, recalling the Jacobean splendor of the Great Hall at Hatfield House, a 17th-century English estate that Mr. Vanderbilt visited with Hunt during their trip to Europe in 1889. The plaster ceiling is webbed with intricate strapwork, the cornice frieze is marked with repeating coats of arms, and the walls are clad with exquisitely carved oak paneling.

The setting is complemented by the stately furnishings, which include several remarkable case pieces. In the corner is a carved ebony cabinet-on-stand made in Antwerp in the 1600s whose inlaid parquetry doors open to reveal a classically inspired architectural scene. Resembling a miniature loggia, it is decorated with a patterned floor, marbleized columns, and gilt-trimmed statuary and overlooks a trompe-l'oeil landscape painting.

The room also features two portraits by Sargent. On the right, in a black dress, is Virginia Purdy Bacon, a cousin and close friend of Mr. Vanderbilt's; on the left is Mrs. Benjamin Kissam, his aunt.

Bronzes

Of the more than 40 bronze sculptures on display at Biltmore, about half are pieces created by les Animaliers—a 19th-century French school of art so called because its adherents specialized in naturalistic depictions of animals. The leader of the group was Antoine-Louis Barye, who is considered one of the finest animal sculptors in history. Mr. Vanderbilt had seen Barye's work in Paris and acquired a number of his sculptures, including the striking Hippogriff seen in the Entrance Hall. Throughout the House are also pieces by Pierre-Jules Mène, whose stag (above left) exemplifies the artist's skill in portraying a moment of an animal's life in the wild; August Nicholas Cain, who crafted these candlesticks (left) ornamented with bird nests; and Jean-François-Théodore Gechter, who was known for his horse figures, such as this horse spooked by a snake (below).

MRS. VANDERBILT'S BEDROOM This graceful, feminine room was designed as a counterpart to Mr. Vanderbilt's Bedroom. When he was still a bachelor, the room was used by his mother, Maria Louisa Kissam Vanderbilt, during her visits to the Estate. After Mr. Vanderbilt married, it became the private quarters of Edith Stuyvesant Dresser Vanderbilt.

Like her husband, Edith Vanderbilt was a member of a prominent family. She counted among her ancestors Peter Stuyvesant, who had been the first governor of Dutch colonial New York in the mid-17th century, and several respected senators, judges, and mayors. Orphaned at a young age, Edith Dresser lived with her aunt and sisters primarily in Paris and, according to contemporary accounts, was considered "a very charming young lady" and "the perfection of hostesses."

Her courtship with George Vanderbilt began in Paris in 1896; they had already known one another for several years. The couple were engaged in April 1898 and wed in a simple ceremony, attended by 150 family members and friends, at the American Cathedral in that city two months later.

When they arrived at the Estate in October, after their honeymoon in Europe, Mrs. Vanderbilt saw her room just as it appears today. The oval-shaped space is decorated in the Louis XV style, which originated in France around 1700 and was adopted by affluent Americans in the late 1800s. The room incorporates such hallmarks of this luxurious style as silk wall covering, fancily trimmed mirrors, Savonnerie carpets, and cut-velvet draperies on the windows and bed. While the two marble-topped commodes are French period pieces, the chairs and chaise are in the Louis XV Revival style, which is typified by white frames, carved floral motifs, and curving profiles. Complementing the look is a collection of French and German prints from the 18th century and a Louis XV clock elaborately embellished with porcelain figurines and flowers.

OPPOSITE: *The sumptuous cut velvet used for the draperies and upholstery in* **Mrs. Vanderbilt's Bedroom** *is a duplicate of the original fabric. It was woven for the restoration of the room in 1990 by Tassinari & Chatel, which retained the loom pattern from which the material had been made a century ago.* LEFT ABOVE: *A gracious, charming woman, Mrs. Vanderbilt was the well-loved chatelaine of Biltmore.* LEFT BELOW: *Mrs. Vanderbilt was a devoted mother to her only daughter, Cornelia, seen here around age 5, who often accompanied her on weekly visits to families living on the Estate.*

*L*IKE THE SECOND FLOOR, THE THIRD FLOOR FEA-
tures a number of spacious guest rooms—each one decorated in a
different style, as was fashionable in the late 19th century—and
also includes a centrally located sitting area. The rooms here were removed from the
bustle of the first floor, but they would still have been occupied by honored guests, whose
names were written on little cards posted on each door—lest visitors lose their way
among the 19 bedrooms that were originally on this level.

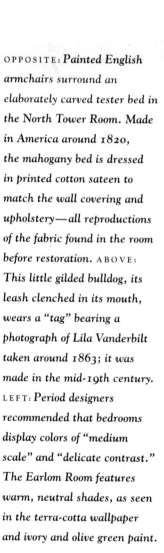

NORTH TOWER ROOM These elegant
guest quarters are part of a suite of four inter-
connected rooms that were opened in April
1995 after two years of exhaustive research and
renovation. Given their grand size and prominent location—directly above the Vanderbilts'
own bedrooms and sitting area—the guest rooms
probably were among the most elaborate in the
house and were reserved for special visitors. It is
believed that the suite would have been shared
by a family.

The North Tower Room, shaped in a graceful oval, is decorated in the dignified Regency
style, which was in vogue in early 19th-century
England and influenced by ancient Greek and
Roman design. Characteristic of the style are the
delicate armchairs, with their attenuated frame

and painted finish, and the languorous chaise
longue, whose lion's-paw feet are modeled on a
classical motif.

EARLOM ROOM This room was inspired
by nine prints in Mr. Vanderbilt's collection
from the English engraver Richard Earlom
(1745–1822). Centerpieces among the eclectic
array of furnishings are an armoire and a fall-
front bombé bureau—both mid-18th-century
examples of Dutch cabinetmakers' command
of exacting marquetry decoration. The silk-
screened, tone-on-tone wallpaper is an exact
reproduction of the original, and the cotton cut
velvet used for the upholstery, bedspread, and
draperies was duplicated from fabric found on
the suite of five Spanish Revival chairs placed
around the room.

OPPOSITE: *Painted English
armchairs surround an
elaborately carved tester bed in
the North Tower Room. Made
in America around 1820,
the mahogany bed is dressed
in printed cotton sateen to
match the wall covering and
upholstery—all reproductions
of the fabric found in the room
before restoration.* ABOVE:
*This little gilded bulldog, its
leash clenched in its mouth,
wears a "tag" bearing a
photograph of Lila Vanderbilt
taken around 1863; it was
made in the mid-19th century.*
LEFT: *Period designers
recommended that bedrooms
display colors of "medium
scale" and "delicate contrast."
The Earlom Room features
warm, neutral shades, as seen
in the terra-cotta wallpaper
and ivory and olive green paint.*

RAPHAEL ROOM As in the Earlom Room, the Raphael Room was designed around a series of prints—in this case 18th- and 19th-century engravings after paintings by the Renaissance master Raphael Sanzio (1483–1520). The 14 artworks, which were executed by several European printmakers, depict the range of subjects for which Raphael is famous, including images of the Madonna and the Holy Family and figures from Christianity and classical mythology.

In contrast to the intricate engravings is the room's understated decor. The wallpaper displays a subtle pattern, the English and American 19th-century furniture boasts little ornamentation beyond its mahogany veneer, and the fabric is a plain cotton velveteen. The simple, refined appearance of this bedroom reflects both the late 19th-century trend toward less cluttered interiors—a reaction against the excessive opulence of the early Victorian era—and the restrained style that arbiters of taste considered appropriate for country retreats.

SOUTH TOWER ROOM Pastel colors and dainty floral-printed fabric mark the South Tower Room, a large, round space decorated in a subdued neoclassical style. The striated wallpaper was adapted from a pattern by William Morris (1834–96), a leading English proponent of "aesthetic" handcrafted design, and is complemented by mauve and ivory trim—the original woodwork colors, which were discovered under a subsequent layer of paint.

Much of the furniture, such as the white bed with caned head- and footboards, the center table, the inlaid commode, and the painted desk, are from late 19th-century France. The remaining pieces, including a suite of Cuban mahogany ballroom chairs, were made primarily in England between the late 1700s and early 1900s. In addition to the blue satin covering the sidechair and seat cushions, a striped cotton fabric was used for the draperies, bed furnishings, and upholstery; it was custom matched to the original fabric on the tufted sofa.

INSET, RIGHT: *This diminutive railcar, complete with couplers and curtains, was made by the French cristallerie Baccarat around 1890 as a carriage for perfume flasks; the cushions at each end were designed for storing hat pins.* BELOW: *Crafted in France in the 19th century, this ornate "toy" furniture—measuring only four inches tall—is hand painted with pastoral scenes.*

ABOVE: *The blue-and-yellow color scheme of the Raphael Room was popular in the 19th century, with blue especially favored to complement the ruddy tones of mahogany, seen here in the sleigh bed and cupboard secretary.*

LEFT: *Indicative of the attention paid to every detail during renovation is the variety of textile trims used in the South Tower Room. Four different types of fringe and 40 tassels were chosen to coordinate with the satin and cotton fabrics.*

THIRD FLOOR LIVING HALL The primary "living room" for visitors staying in the upper guest wing, the Third Floor Living Hall was intended for relaxing and socializing. In this informal meeting area, houseguests could take tea, match wits over parlor games, curl up with an engaging book, or be entertained by the player piano. The area is now used periodically for special exhibitions.

The room, replete with art objects in diverse media, gives ample evidence of Mr. Vanderbilt's passion for collecting—a passion he inherited from his father. William Henry was renown for his treasure-filled mansion on 640 Fifth Avenue, which housed thousands of porcelains, metalworks, crystal pieces, silverwares, tapestries, sculptures, and paintings; indeed, his collection was so extensive that documenting it required a four-volume catalog.

The three glass-front curio cabinets in the Living Hall originally stood in William Henry's dining room. These massive oak pieces now contain a variety of European and Oriental ceramics, including decorative plates, hollowware, and porcelain figurines. Atop the tables are bronze statuary and marble portrait busts, along with several pairs of ornamental candlesticks in brass, porcelain, or wood.

On the walls are 19th-century portrait prints taken from paintings by Sir Joshua Reynolds and architectural prints by Axel Haig (1835–1921), the noted Swedish etcher. Haig had been an architect, and many of his compositions depict cathedrals and other large structures.

Of special interest are the two photogravures of female figures hanging beside the fireplace. They are the work of James Whistler, a distinguished printmaker as well as a painter whose style was influenced by Japanese art. He was a close friend of the Vanderbilts', who corresponded with the artist and invited him to stay at their Paris apartment during a visit in 1902; Mr. Vanderbilt served as a pallbearer at Whistler's funeral the following year.

OPPOSITE: *The canvas on view on the easel depicts one of William Henry Vanderbilt's merchant vessels.* ABOVE: *The side-drummer is one of more than 20 porcelain musicians in the Affenkapelle, or monkey band—a comical series made by Meissen in the 1800s.*

Orientalia

After Japan opened its border in 1854, the country became the source of much fascination for Westerners, touching off a craze for Eastern decorative styles and objects. Mr. Vanderbilt traveled to Japan in October and November 1892 and was so taken with its artworks that he sent back to Biltmore some 300 artifacts, such as armor, ceramics, kimonos, and netsuke (small, carved ornaments). In the 32-case shipment was an 18th-century incense burner (right) of Satsuma ware, a gaudily decorated type of pottery made on Kyushu island. Also included was a daishō (above)—a set of short and long swords like those worn by samurai in the 1600s through mid-1800s; the scabbards and stand are elaborately adorned with lacquer.

Please continue down the Grand Staircase to the Second Floor.

SHERATON ROOM This elegant, sophisticated room is named for one of the foremost English cabinetmakers, Thomas Sheraton (1751–1806). His furniture designs, published in three widely read pattern books, were influential in the development of neoclassical decorating styles at the turn of the 19th century.

It would have been popular at the time to use wall coverings and fabrics in muted tones, as seen here in the soft peach wallpaper, bed hangings, and window draperies. Also representative of the style is the fireplace mantel, which is carved with such neoclassical motifs as medallions, urns, and swags.

The English satinwood and mahogany furniture pieces in the Sheraton style—including a double desk, square-back sofa, and nightstand—are typically light and delicate, with tapered legs and graceful silhouettes. Of particular note is the tester bed, which is painted with bows, cherubs, and beribboned flower garlands; it is similar to a design in one of Sheraton's books.

Over the fireplace is a portrait of George Vanderbilt and his siblings Frederick and Lila as children; George, the dark-haired boy on the left, would have been five years old when he sat for the artist Jacob H. Lazarus (1822–91) in 1867. On the other side of the doorway is another "portrait"—the Currier & Ives print depicts William Henry Vanderbilt racing his famous trotters, Aldine and Maud S. (the latter bought for $20,000 in 1878).

RIGHT: *The satinwood tester bed in the Sheraton Room is elegantly draped with peach silk hangings. The piece is based on a plate (above) in Thomas Sheraton's first pattern book,* The Cabinet-Maker and Upholsterer's Drawing Book, *published between 1791 and 1794; an original copy of this volume can be found in the Library.*

CHIPPENDALE ROOM Like the Sheraton Room, this guest room reflects the popularity of an important English furniture maker. Thomas Chippendale (1718–79) was the first to bring out a pattern book devoted entirely to furniture. In *The Gentleman and Cabinet-Maker's Director*, published in 1754, he presented a range of elaborate designs adapted from the Louis XV style and thereby influenced the fashion for fancy interiors.

Exemplifying the Chippendale style are the tester bed and seating furniture, which were made in 18th- and 19th-century England. These mahogany pieces include such typical stylistic elements as curved cabriole legs, hairy paw feet, and carved leaf and shell motifs. Also in keeping with the period is the use of coordinating wallpaper and fabrics.

ABOVE: *The leaded-glass firescreen in the Chippendale Room was given to Hunt by the construction crew that worked on Biltmore House.*
RIGHT: The Young Algerian Girl *is one of two paintings in the room by Pierre-Auguste Renoir (1841–1919), a leading French Impressionist whose work first became popular in America at the turn of the century.*

OLD ENGLISH ROOM Decorated in the Jacobean style, this room provides an appropriate setting for the suite of upholstered seating pieces, which are reproductions of 17th-century furniture at Knole in Kent, England. The novel designs feature mechanical parts that can be adjusted by ratchets, which allow the sofa, for example, to be converted into a daybed.

On display are several Cecil family portraits. Over the mantel is the Great Lord Burghley, William Cecil; above the oak chest are his grandchildren William and Frances, painted in 1599 by the Italian artist Frederico Zuccaro (1543–1609). Between the two 16th-century portraits is their descendant, the Honorable John Francis Amherst Cecil, who married George Vanderbilt's daughter, Cornelia, in 1924.

ABOVE LEFT: *Among the family likenesses in the 17th-century-style Old English Room are William and Frances Cecil (left) and Lord Burghley (above right), who was a principal minister to Queen Elizabeth I between 1558 and his death in 1598. The latter portrait was done in 1589 by the Flemish painter Marcus Gheeraerts the Younger (1561–1636), a favorite artist of English royalty.*

*T*HE DOWNSTAIRS LEVEL OF BILTMORE HOUSE SERVED three distinct purposes. It contained the recreation areas that were used by the Vanderbilts and their guests. It also housed the bedrooms and common rooms for the "below stairs" staff. And, as was customary in great country estates, the basement accommodated the pantries and service areas, designed to keep kitchen and laundry clamor far removed from the living quarters upstairs.

HALLOWEEN ROOM This one-time storage area was taken over in 1924 by Cornelia and John Cecil and their guests for a party during their wedding festivities. Each guest personally designed a different section on the walls, thus creating the unusual decoration. The space is now used for changing exhibits on the history, collections, and preservation of the Estate.

BOWLING ALLEY The sport of bowling arrived in America in the 1600s with the Dutch settlers and had become a popular pastime by the 1800s, as Victorian men patronized an ever-increasing number of public lanes. At Biltmore both men and women played on one of the first bowling alleys in a private home. The lanes were installed in 1895 by the Brunswick-Balke-Collender Company, a top manufacturer of recreation equipment, and were constructed just as alleys are today. Durable maple planks were laid along the first third of the lanes, which takes the most wear from balls striking the surface, and softer pine decking was used on the remainder, where the balls roll. Balls were returned and pins reset by hand.

DRESSING ROOMS Among affluent Victorians, each activity had its own dress code, for which ladies and gentlemen might have to change their clothes several times a day. To change for recreation, guests used the Dressing Rooms, which were arrayed along separate halls for men and women. These private chambers guaranteed that no one would have to make a long, potentially embarrassing trip from bedroom to basement immodestly attired.

OPPOSITE: *Wooden balls of different sizes indicate that a variety of games besides tenpins could be played in the Bowling Alley.* LEFT: *In the main Dressing Room, Cornelia Vanderbilt's ivory grooming set is displayed on a 19th-century English mahogany table; a wooden towel rack holds fresh linens.* ABOVE: *This figure is part of the imaginative mural painted for a party in the Halloween Room in 1924.*

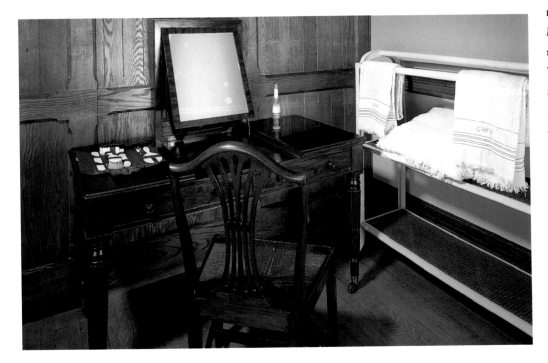

SWIMMING POOL Biltmore offered a wide range of recreational activities—reflecting not only the need for entertainment in a remote mountain region but also the new emphasis placed on health, fitness, and exercise in the late 1800s. Among the most popular diversions was bathing, which lured Victorians to seashore and lakeside resorts each summer.

The Vanderbilts and their guests, however, could enjoy the water in any season—in a 70,000-gallon indoor pool. Measuring 53 feet long by 27 feet wide by 8½ feet deep, the tile-work pool was equipped with such amenities as underwater lighting, safety ropes, and a diving platform. Although unheated, it was fed with hot water through the black hose; the large standing pipe supplied cold water.

Illuminated by chandeliers, the room is also one of the best places to see the fireproof, terra-cotta tile vaulting that appears in several areas of the House. The vaults were installed according to a technologically advanced building system developed by Rafael Guastavino; his technique was favored by architects because it allowed masonry vaulting to cover wide spans without needing interior supports during construction.

GYMNASIUM While both men and women used the Swimming Pool—albeit at separate times—the Gymnasium was primarily a male precinct. Here guests could tone their muscles with the most up-to-date apparatus, including parallel bars, a chain-driven rowing machine, and wall-mounted pulleys with adjustable weights. The gym also offered barbells, medicine balls, Indian clubs (used to improve hand-eye coordination), and, for the refined athlete, a fencing set. After a vigorous workout, guests could cool down in the showers.

LEFT: Men and women swam in the pool separately, as dictated by contemporary mores. Both sexes would have worn bathing costumes that reached down to the knee and up to the neck. INSET, OPPOSITE: Much of the 19th-century equipment in the Gymnasium, including the exercise machines, parallel bars, and Indian clubs, was manufactured by A. G. Spalding & Bro., which is still a prominent sporting-goods company today.

PANTRIES Accommodating the large number of family members, guests, and staff at Biltmore required an extensive larder—especially when provisions were bought in bulk. One bill of sale from 1896, for example, records an order for 28 pounds of lamb legs and loins, 52 pounds of prime beef ribs, 22 broiling and roasting chickens, 62 pounds of muskmelons, and two baskets of peaches.

Groceries from shops in Asheville's Central Market, as well as fresh produce, meats, and dairy products from Biltmore's farm operation, were kept in a series of pantries. The Vegetable Pantry held bins of fruits and vegetables; the Small Pantry stored canned goods; the Housekeeper's Pantry also had canned goods, along with a desk used by the head housekeeper; and the Canning Pantry would

have contained produce put up on the Estate.

WALK-IN REFRIGERATORS Perishables were preserved in two spacious walk-in food lockers that were cooled by a chilled brine solution circulating through pipes in their interiors. Any sort of refrigeration, let alone cold storage on this scale, was a novelty in the late 1800s, when most homes still relied on iceboxes and springhouses.

SERVANTS' BEDROOMS At any one time 80 servants might be employed at Biltmore, where they lived near their work stations in separate halls according to sex and "rank." The bedrooms along this corridor represent the private quarters for female members of the staff, which included cooks, house maids, and scullery maids. The rooms are airy and comfortable, with splint-seat chairs, chestnut dressers and wardrobes, and

iron beds and washstands holding monogrammed chamber sets.

On display is some of the original livery used by staff members, whose service dress changed with their job and the time of day. The maids, for instance, wore pink uniforms with white collars and cuffs in the morning and black with white trim in the evening; a cook's helper wore a red-checked pinafore and a dust cap.

Mounted on the wall outside the bedrooms is one of several call boxes found throughout the House. It is part of an ingenious electric communication system that enabled servants to be summoned with a mere touch of a button from most of the upstairs rooms. The boxes registered a call by ringing a bell and raising a little arrow that indicated the room from which it originated.

OPPOSITE TOP: *The spacious Housekeeper's Pantry doubled as a storage area and an office for the head housekeeper, whose job entailed inventorying and replenishing supplies.*
OPPOSITE BOTTOM: *Walk-in food lockers stored the quantities of food required for Biltmore's large household.*

ABOVE: *One of more than 60 staff rooms, this simply furnished Servant's Bedroom includes a cast-iron bed and washstand. Such inexpensive pieces were first made in the mid-1800s and soon became popular among health-conscious Victorians, who believed that metal, unlike wood, did not harbor germs.*

PASTRY KITCHEN Biltmore's kitchen complex, comparable in size to that of a large hotel, was designed for maximum efficiency in food preparation and service. Cooking chores were carried out in three specialized areas, each finished with tiled floors and walls for easy maintenance and each fully stocked with the latest culinary equipment. Staffed by a small army of chefs, cooks, and maids, the kitchens turned out everything from a cup of tea to the lavish banquets that were in vogue at the turn of the century; indeed, a formal dinner could include up to 20 courses and last for several hours.

The Pastry Kitchen was used for fine baking and provided all manner of breads and rich confections beloved by Victorians (a 19th-century cookbook might list hundreds of recipes for cakes and pies). Dough was rolled out on the marble-topped table built in beneath the window; stone slabs like this are preferred by bakers because dough is less likely to stick to the surface. Pastries were baked in two ovens, and dough and finished baked goods were kept chilled in a refrigerator.

ROTISSERIE KITCHEN Another cooking area is the Rotisserie Kitchen, which was used for roasting meat, poultry, and game. Such foods—especially pheasant, duck, venison, and other animals brought back from shooting parties—figured heavily on period menus, often being served for several courses in the same meal.

The iron rotisserie oven, fueled by wood or coal, features a mechanized rotary spit whose speed can be regulated by the electric rheostat mounted on the wall. A drip pan caught grease spatters, and a large overhead vent hood drew off smoke.

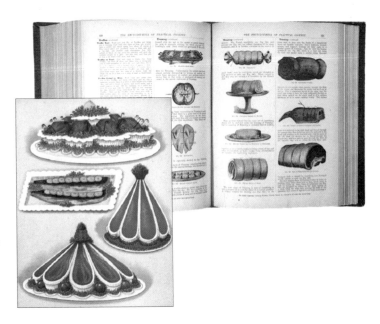

OPPOSITE: *While bread was sometimes ordered from the French Bakery in Asheville, most baked goods served on Biltmore's tables were made in the Pastry Kitchen.* ABOVE: *Meats were roasted over an open fire in the rotisserie oven.* LEFT: The Encyclopædia of Practical Cookery, *part of Biltmore's book collection, was published in London around 1893; it offers instruction on trussing meat and suggestions for "artistic" supper dishes.*

ABOVE: *The Main Kitchen is well stocked with such tools of the chef's trade as copper cookware, knives, sharpening steels, and choppers. The silverplate serving trolley, fitted with chafing dishes, was used to transport hot foods to the upstairs dining rooms.*

OPPOSITE TOP: *The electric dumbwaiter in the Kitchen Pantry has push-button controls and runs 38 feet between the basement and second floor.*

OPPOSITE BOTTOM: *This hand-cranked, tin "chopping machine" was the 19th-century equivalent of a food processor.*

MAIN KITCHEN Most of the cooking at Biltmore took place in the roomy Main Kitchen. Work here started early each morning, when the scullery maid stoked the firebox of the cast-iron cookstove with wood or coal; then the kitchen staff set the work table with knives, choppers, cleavers, braising mallets, and other utensils for the chefs. At hand overhead is a battery of polished copper pots and pans—considered the

for hot coals, while the top section—which has doors that slide upward to help prevent burned elbows—held trays of food. This device was essential for keeping food at the proper temperature so that a large number of diners could be served at the same time.

KITCHEN PANTRY Meals prepared in the basement kitchens had to be transported to the first-floor Butler's Pantry, outside the Banquet Hall, where they were transferred onto serving dishes. (The servants responsible for this chore were familiarly called "tweenies," as they brought food between the kitchens and dining rooms.) While a warming cart was often used for carrying food, meals could be sent upstairs from the Kitchen Pantry via two dumbwaiters— one manual, one electric; the latter had a lifting capacity of 250 pounds and an operating speed of 100 feet per minute. This room was also used for storing the servants' china and washing dishes.

premier cookware for its ability to conduct and retain heat evenly. And displayed around the room are such vintage gadgets as a coffee mill and sausage stuffer; in the corner is an outsized mortar and pestle.

On one side of the stove, which is seven and a half feet long, is a small, separate grill and on the other is a tall iron "cabinet" used as a food warmer: the bottom cupboards hold trays

SERVANTS' DINING ROOM The domestic staff at Biltmore was ordered in a strict hierarchy, as was traditional in the late 1800s. The chef, butler, housekeeper, valet, and lady's maid were among the upper servants, while the footman, page, maid-of-all-work, and scullery maid were considered the lower servants. The groups rarely ate or socialized together, however. In the Servants' Dining Room, which was one of several areas used for staff meals, the servants ate in shifts, with the senior staff taking their place at the table first—cooked for and waited on by the lower-ranking staff.

SERVANTS' SITTING ROOM Like the upstairs Living Halls used by family and guests, this room functioned as a gathering place for staff passing the time or waiting to work. Here they might have read, written letters, played cards, or listened to the Victrola.

TRUNK ROOM The Vanderbilts, like many well-to-do families of their era, were frequent travelers who required a number of huge trunks—packed with at least four changes of clothing for each day—on their months-long trips. The Trunk Room was used for storing luggage for family and guests.

WORK ROOM This room is used by the floral design staff to prepare the cut-flower arrangements seen throughout the House. Plants from the gardens and greenhouses have always played an important role in the decor at Biltmore.

OPPOSITE: *Staff ate in the Servants' Dining Room around a mahogany dining table, seated on bentwood chairs. On the oak sideboard at the rear of the room is a brass table gong that Mr. Vanderbilt bought in 1896 in London; such gongs were used to summon servants.*

ABOVE: *Servants used this sitting room in their free time to write letters on an oak desk, made by Biltmore Industries, or play records on the early 20th-century RCA Victrola.*
RIGHT: *This Autoharp, a zither-like instrument used to accompany singing, was made by the Zimmerman Autoharp Company, Dolgeville, New York.*

BROWN LAUNDRY Like the kitchens, Biltmore's laundry complex was a convenient, efficient operation organized on a commercial scale. In four specialized work rooms the laundress and maids handled the substantial quantities of clothing and linens generated by family, guests, and servants.

The Brown Laundry was used for staff laundry and hand washables and is equipped with deep tubs in which dirt was laboriously scrubbed away on fluted-tin washboards. The wooden "cradle" is a hand-agitated mechanical washing machine from the early 1900s. On the table are various pressing devices, including fluting irons with ridged rollers for crimping pleats and ruffles and double-pointed sadirons that were heated on a special laundry stove. Next door is the Laundresses' Toilet, which was for staff use.

MAIN LAUNDRY The equipment in the Main Laundry is similar to the state-of-the-art machinery originally installed in 1895. In addition to a belt-driven barrel washer are an extractor, which was used to wring out excess water, and a mangle, which was used for pressing.

DRYING ROOM On the right side of the Main Laundry is the Drying Room; all laundry was dried indoors, so that the laundress would never be at the mercy of the weather. After the laundry was wrung as dry as possible, it was draped over an innovative system of rolling wooden racks that could be pulled out from a wall cabinet for air drying or pushed back into niches that were heated with electric coils running along the floor.

OPPOSITE: *Linens aired on pull-out racks, which could be slid into recesses in a wall cabinet where heat from floor-mounted electric coils speeded drying.* INSET, LEFT: *This sadiron, made by the Enterprise Manufacturing Company of Philadelphia, features a detachable stay-cool wooden handle that could be used interchangeably on iron bodies kept heating on a laundry stove.* BELOW: *In the Brown Laundry hand washing was done with wooden washboards in the enameled basins.*

ET OFF FROM THE REST OF THE FIRST FLOOR IS the Bachelors' Wing, a private, all-male haven that had its own entrance—through a covered carriage porch off the stable court-yard—and was connected to the single men's upstairs guest rooms by a separate stair-well. It also boasted specialized game and sitting areas where gentlemen, away from the eyes and ears of the ladies, could discuss business and politics (subjects then considered beyond the ken of women), relax with a pipe, or relive exploits from a day's shooting party.

OPPOSITE: *With its ebonized woodwork and gold-leaf wall covering, the Gun Room is a handsome showcase for hunting trophies, such as this game bird (above), and sporting art. The room also displayed guns; collecting antique and contemporary firearms was a favorite gentlemen's pastime in the Victorian era.* RIGHT: *In turn-of-the-century society, smoking was an acceptable practice—for men at least— as long as it was done in a separate room. The Smoking Room provided a comfortable retreat for male guests to enjoy an after-dinner cigar.*

SMOKING ROOM Smoking, like gambling and hunting, was primarily a male prerogative in the 1800s, and the smoking parlor became a required feature in fashionable country houses soon after it appeared in mid-century. Once the women had gone to bed, men donned elaborate smoking jackets and savored the pleasure of a cigar or pipe, perhaps as an accompaniment to a glass of after-dinner spirits; they might even try the new machine-rolled cigarettes being produced in the tobacco centers of North Carolina. Guests could also select a leather-bound book from the collection and read before the fire in the plush 17th-century-style sofas and chairs.

GUN ROOM Male guests at Biltmore never wanted for outdoor recreation. There was horse-back riding, carriage driving, fishing, hiking, and, of course, hunting—the quintessential country house amusement. To insure a good day's shooting, Mr. Vanderbilt had the Estate stocked with a plentiful supply of deer, quail, pheasant, and other wild game.

The Gun Room pays tribute to the popularity of the sport, which had developed into such a passion by the 1870s that the proper house was considered incomplete without this special shrine. As was customary, the room is outfitted with glass-front cases for firearms, which were stored in custom-built racks, and for an array of animal trophies. On the walls are 19th-century prints with a sporting theme by the British artists Sir Joshua Reynolds and James Ward (1769–1859), and on the tables are bronze sculptures of game animals and a hunting dog.

HOUSE AS LARGE AND COMPLEX AS BILTMORE could operate only with an efficient (and mostly invisible) infrastructure—from the boilers that fired the central heating system to the sizable storage area that held the china. The Behind-the-Scenes Tour is a special guided tour, available by reservation only, that offers a chance to view the inner workings of this busy household, as well as to visit rooms that are not regularly open.

UPPER FLOORS The tour begins with the second- and third-floor guest wing, where several bedrooms and bathrooms—still decorated with their original paint and wallpaper—await restoration. In these rooms are stored many of the furnishings that Mr. Vanderbilt acquired for the House. The fourth floor features servants' bedrooms and the two-story Observatory that Mrs. Vanderbilt and her daughter used as an art studio.

MAIDS' SITTING ROOM Located on a landing between the second and third floors, this room served as a gathering place for Biltmore's servants and those traveling with guests. Women could spend a spare moment here socializing, reading, sewing, or taking a rest between chores.

MRS. VANDERBILT'S BATH AND DRESSING AREA This spacious bath, adjoining Mrs. Vanderbilt's Bedroom, is outfitted with a paw-footed tub and a shower but no sink. Instead, it was deemed proper for a maid to bring the lady of the house a basin of water, along with fresh towels. Mrs. Vanderbilt's linens, many of which were purchased in Paris in the 1890s and are embroidered with her monogram, are stored in cabinets across from her Dressing Area.

ABOVE LEFT: *The Balcony Room, a former guest room on the third floor, is now used for storage.* ABOVE RIGHT: *A pair of rosewood armchairs, in the ornate Rococo Revival style* popular in the mid-1800s, *provides seating in the Maids' Sitting Room.* OPPOSITE: *Still painted in its original soft lilac color, Mrs. Vanderbilt's Bath featured a shower so novel in* the 1890s that operating it *required written instruction. Printed on the enameled faucet facing, the directions read, "2 turns cold, 4 turns mixed, and 6 turns hot."*

ABOVE LEFT: *The Lady's Maid's Room features simple oak furnishings.* ABOVE RIGHT: *The Sewing Room was used for all types of projects — from stitching draperies to darning socks. The Singer sewing machine is from the early 1900s.* INSET, RIGHT: *Once fired by wood and coal, three boilers — each holding 20,000 gallons of water — provided steam heat that could raise room temperature to at least 60 degrees.* OPPOSITE: *Floor-to-ceiling cupboards in the Butler's Pantry hold egg cups, cheese bells, jelly molds, cake stands, and other pieces used in cooking and dining.*

LADY'S MAID'S ROOM As was customary for women of her social standing, Mrs. Vanderbilt employed a lady's maid, who tended to her personal effects, assisted her in dressing, helped her manage the household, and accompanied her when traveling. This was a prestigious position in the hierarchy of servants, earning the lady's maid the only staff bedroom on the second floor; it is located next to Mrs. Vanderbilt's quarters. The room is a bit larger than those of the other servants and is furnished with simple oak pieces that were mass-manufactured at the turn of the century.

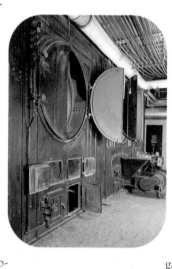

SEWING ROOM It was in the Sewing Room that the house seamstress would call together female servants to sew upholstery, bedding, and draperies and to work on routine mending and darning. Besides doing handwork, servants could use a Singer treadle-powered sewing machine, which was especially convenient for making staff uniforms. The floor was left bare intentionally — so that dropped needles, pins, and bits of thread could easily be spotted and retrieved.

BUTLER'S PANTRY On the ground floor is the Butler's Pantry, where tableware is stored. Meals brought up from the kitchens were placed on serving pieces here and delivered to the dining rooms; food could be kept hot in the iron warmer under the counter. A speaking tube on the end wall allowed communication with the Main Kitchen, while the call box outside the room was used to signal staff.

SUB-BASEMENT A look at 19th-century technology is given in the sub-basement, where the original heating and power equipment still stand. In addition to the boilers are the gas-powered dynamo that generated some of the electricity for the House and the main electrical switchboard. Nearby were the 300-pound mechanized ice maker and the refrigeration plant, which pumped a brine solution chilled by compressed ammonia gas to individual coolers in the kitchen and pantry areas.

*I*N THE PREAUTOMOTIVE AGE OF THE LATE 19TH century, horses and horse-drawn vehicles played an important role in both transportation and recreation. Reflecting their significance is the 12,000-square-foot stable complex at the north end of the front facade— a facility that was as carefully designed and completely equipped as the House itself.

STABLE Like his father, who was so devoted to his trotters that he built an indoor riding ring for them, Mr. Vanderbilt took exceptional care of his horses. As many as 25 riding and driving horses, along with 20 carriages, were sheltered at Biltmore in a modern stable complete with electricity, plumbing, glazed-brick walls, and brass fixtures and hardware.

The Stable also contained all the attendant service areas, including rooms for saddles, tack, harness, blankets, and feed, as well as the Estate offices and living quarters for single male servants. Among the staff of about 25 stable hands were grooms, a harness man, an exerciser,

and a coachman, whose job entailed supervising the grooming of the horses, driving family and guests in the carriages, and assisting riders with their mounts.

Today the Stable has been converted into an avenue of shops offering books, confections, toys, Christmas ornaments, and decorative accessories. The largest shop is located in the former Carriage House, while a café now occupies the old horse stable—with tables tucked into the original box stalls. In the courtyard, where horses' hooves and carriage wheels once clattered on the brick pavers, tables and chairs are set out for dining or relaxing in the historic setting.

ABOVE: *The Stable was still under construction in the spring of 1894. On Olmsted's advice, it was located at the north end of the House to buffer the gardens from wind.* RIGHT: *Riders posed on their mounts on the Front Lawn* around 1900. OPPOSITE: *Horses and carriages would arrive in the Stable courtyard through the arched Porte Cochere. On the center dormer is a "master" clock, which electrically controls the clocks in the servants' quarters.*

Biltmore Gardens

From mountain forest to mani-

cured flower bed to valley farm, the grounds

at Biltmore were unparalleled in scale and

diversity when conceived in the 1880s. They

remain one of the premier achievements of

America's foremost landscape architect, Fred-

erick Law Olmsted. His genius for design and

his love of nature are visible today throughout

the 8,000-acre Estate, where his plan and many

of the original plants have been preserved.

*W*HAT IS NOW A LUSH, MATURE LANDSCAPE WAS once a depleted tract that could support neither farm nor forest. Olmsted transformed the site with a series of gardens designed to complement the architecture of the House, take advantage of the native flora and terrain, and provide varied settings for outdoor recreation. Beginning with the formal lawns around the House, the grounds become increasingly naturalistic as they spread out toward a managed woodland that looks so wild it appears never to have been touched.

APPROACH ROAD An integral part of Biltmore's landscape is the three-mile-long Approach Road. It begins at the Lodge Gate, the pebbledash gatehouse at the edge of Biltmore Village, and ends at the sphinx-topped stone pillars near the Front Lawn. In between it traverses a "garden" as meticulously planned as the formal flower beds.

Olmsted designed the Approach Road to heighten anticipation of seeing the House by having visitors first wind slowly through a woodland. The idea, he said, was to evoke a sense of mystery while creating the " . . . sensation of passing through the remote depths of a natural forest." And so the drive snakes along the ravines through dense border plantings of rhododendron, mountain laurel, and azalea, passing from woods to open meadow and back again to groves of hemlock and pine—with no distant views to interrupt the intimate effect. At every turn is a new surprise: a stream, a pool, a blanket of wildflowers, a thicket of river cane.

In developing this "natural" landscape, Olmsted started virtually from scratch, sculpting the land before installing any plant material. Many of the trees and shrubs he used were transplants collected as seedlings from the Carolina plains, piedmont, and mountains. These native specimens were supplemented with plants grown in Biltmore's own nursery, which had been established in 1889 with stock and seeds from the acclaimed Arnold Arboretum near Boston, as well as from other nurseries in America and Europe.

Because the family traveled frequently— "Mr. Vanderbilt and his guests always miss the best of the bloom," lamented Olmsted—the Approach Road was planted with a variety of deciduous trees, conifers, and flowering shrubs that would provide interest year-round. There were even exotic species, such as bamboo, to add a subtropical character to the landscape. The design was acknowledged to be a success, even by so particular a critic as Richard Morris Hunt. "Hasn't Olmsted done wonders with the approach road?" he wrote in an 1892 letter to Mr. Vanderbilt. "It alone will give him lasting fame."

OPPOSITE: Designed by Hunt, the Lodge Gate was built with bricks and roof tiles made on the Estate; it is faced with a rough stucco finish called pebbledash. BOTTOM: *Mr. Vanderbilt, standing beside Olmsted (far right, front row), poses with the crew during construction of the Approach Road in 1892.* INSET, BELOW: *The drive is lined with dense border plantings to create a mysterious, intimate effect.*

ESPLANADE At the end of the Approach Road, Biltmore House at last comes into view, rising before a trim, level lawn lined with double rows of tulip trees. The contrast in style between the naturalistic drive and the formal grounds immediately surrounding the House is deliberate: Olmsted used this area to form a transition between the stately building and the wilder, outlying landscape.

The entire forecourt is called the Esplanade and was inspired by the gardens at the mid-17th-century Château de Vaux-le-Vicomte near Melun, France. It incorporates the Front Lawn, with its softly splashing fountain, and the majestic Rampe Douce (meaning "gentle incline"), a graduated stairway zigzagging along a rough-cut limestone wall. Beyond stretches a grassy slope known as the Vista, with a statue of Diana, goddess of the hunt, marking the summit—the perfect vantage point for viewing the House against its backdrop of mountains.

TERRACES Visitors at Biltmore, who would often stay for weeks or months at a time, were encouraged to use the entire landscape—whether by hiking through the forest, playing lawn games, or simply watching the sunset from the comfort of a garden bench. The Terraces were designed for those who preferred to stay close by the House. Guests could enjoy the shade of the Library Terrace, which is sheltered by an arbor of fragrant wisteria and colorful trumpet creeper. Or they might stroll to the South Terrace, once the site of a bowling green, to relax in the limestone teahouse and take in the spectacular panorama of the Deerpark, the Lagoon, and the Blue Ridge Mountains; Mount Pisgah, at 5,800 feet, is the highest peak in the distance.

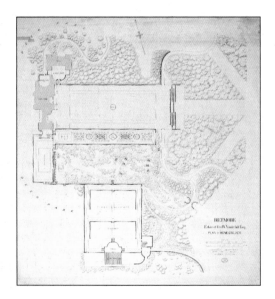

ABOVE LEFT: *Olmsted's original plan for the Home Grounds covered the design for seven garden areas around the House—from the Esplanade to the Walled Garden.*

ABOVE RIGHT: *The Rampe Douce was already completed by December 1892, while the rest of the Esplanade and the House were still under construction.* INSET, ABOVE:

Young Cornelia takes a dip in the Front Lawn fountain in this circa 1910 photo.
OPPOSITE: *The statue of Diana stands before a double grove of hemlock trees that*

seem to form the letter "V"; the Rampe Douce is at the base of the slope. The lawn between was originally mowed by a horse- or mule-drawn tractor fitted with blades.

BELOW: *Water lilies and Egyptian lotus fill the pools in the Italian Garden; in warm weather the bed in the central pool is stocked with cannas and ornamental grasses, both popular in turn-of-the-century gardens.* OPPOSITE: *A path threads past forsythia, pink and white dogwood, holly, and white-flowering crab apple in the Ramble. The garden is so lush and varied that the promenade seems longer than it actually is.*

ITALIAN GARDEN Three symmetrical pools mark the Italian Garden, where gravel paths and manicured lawns form an ordered composition reminiscent of Italian Renaissance landscape design. Enclosed by a hemlock hedge and stone walls, the garden was intended as a separate outdoor "room" and is decorated with classical statuary, jardinieres, and benches. While the space was meant for quiet contemplation, it was also used for recreation: tennis and croquet were played on the grassy area nearest the House. After their game guests could slip into the basement to change through the door under the stairway.

PERGOLA Another broad stone stair leads to the wisteria-covered Pergola overlooking the former lawn tennis court. The shady bower provided a cool spot for spectators, who could also enjoy the soft music of trickling wall fountains.

SHRUB GARDEN In contrast to the formal Italian Garden is the four-acre Shrub Garden, or Ramble—a rich, picturesque landscape with hundreds of woody plants. Olmsted chose this protected site for a "secluded and genial" garden where guests could "ramble" along meandering paths through an ever-changing pageant of plants. Filled with specimens that provide a succession of color—from the winter jasmine that opens in February to the cut-leaf Japanese maples that blush red until frost—this area features such old-fashioned shrubs as lilac, viburnum, forsythia, and honeysuckle. It also includes numerous species native to Asia, such as Japanese stewartia, kousa dogwood, and Yoshino cherry, reflecting the Victorians' interest in plants being introduced from the Far East in the late 1800s.

WALLED GARDEN The gate at the lower edge of the Ramble opens into the four-acre Walled Garden, which Olmsted had initially planned with mixed plots of flowers, fruits, and vegetables typical of an English kitchen garden. Mr. Vanderbilt, however, insisted on a "garden of ornament rather than utility," reasoning that the Estate farm would supply the produce instead.

A 236-foot-long grape arbor entwined with many of the original vines forms the spine of the symmetrical plan, which comprises beds of flowers arranged in tapestry-like patterns, similar to an Elizabethan knot garden. The garden blooms with a progression of color, starting in spring with daffodils, hyacinths, and tulips. These are followed in summer by some 40 varieties of annuals, including dahlias, zinnias, and globe amaranth, while fall brings a multi-hued display of chrysanthemums. Along the outer walls are espaliered fruit trees, rose-of-Sharon, and pyracantha—whose candelabra and fan shapes require trimming at least six times per growing season—as well as perennial borders of bleeding heart, peony, iris, and daylily.

ROSE GARDEN The lower half of the walled area is given over to about 2,000 roses in more than 100 varieties, including All-America Rose Selections. While most of the plants are modern hybrid teas, floribundas, and grandifloras, the garden also boasts a growing number of heirloom roses—especially varieties that were grown for the Vanderbilts, such as Paul Neyron (which was introduced in 1869) and American Beauty (introduced in 1875).

CONSERVATORY Designed by Hunt and rebuilt in 1957, the glass-roofed Conservatory provides flowering and green plants for Biltmore House and tender bedding plants for the gardens—just as it did in the Vanderbilts' day. The central room is still used for raising such large specimens as palm and banana trees; custom-built oversized doors allowed huge potted plants like these to be transferred to the Winter Garden, where they could be properly displayed. The adjoining greenhouse wings are filled with orchids, ferns, succulents, and other hothouse plants.

OPPOSITE: *The Walled Garden is abloom with some 50,000 Dutch tulips in spring. Such enclosed gardens were common in England and northern Europe because they "trapped" sunshine and shielded plants from wind, creating a hospitable microclimate.* INSET, LEFT: *Among the 100 varieties in the Rose Garden is the Pink Peace rose, a fragrant, long-blooming hybrid tea introduced in 1959.* BELOW: *The beds in front of the Conservatory are filled with buddleia, asters, sunflowers, and other colorful plants that attract butterflies.*

SPRING GARDEN Sheltered by a cathedral grove of white pines and hemlocks, the Spring Garden lies in a secluded pocket just beyond the Ramble. The garden was named for the two small springs found here, which Olmsted diverted underground to create a stream flowing into the Azalea Garden. He also called it the Vernal Garden for its spring-blooming shrubs, such as forsythia, spirea, deutzia, and mock orange.

AZALEA GARDEN A wood-chip path connects the Spring Garden to the 20-acre Azalea Garden, the largest and "lowest" of the gardens that occupy a series of hollows below the House. Olmsted called it the Glen, for its protected valley site. Today, however, it is named—and renowned—for its superb array of azaleas.

These plants were assembled by Chauncey Beadle, a Cornell-educated horticulturist who was hired "temporarily" in 1890 to oversee the nursery but stayed on until his death in 1950, eventually becoming estate superintendent. Over the course of 15 years Beadle and three friends, who called themselves the "Azalea Hunters," traveled from New England to Florida to Texas studying and gathering native specimens. In 1940 he donated his entire collection of 3,000 plants—which was one of the largest in the world—to Biltmore Estate.

More than 1,000 azaleas, representing 14 native species and countless hybrids, now thrive in the garden, growing alongside metasequoias, magnolias, dogwoods, and a number of conifers that Beadle added from an arboretum that was never completed. Included in the vast variety of plants are such rarities as the Florida torreya, now facing extinction in its natural habitat, and the Franklinia, which disappeared from the wild in 1790.

OPPOSITE: *The naturalistic Azalea Garden was originally planted with a variety of shrubs, flowers, and ground covers. It now features one of the most complete collections of native azaleas in existence, along with numerous hybrids, such as these Asiatic specimens surrounded by stewartia, hemlock, spruce, and dogwood.* LEFT: *Edged with towering pines and hemlocks, the Spring Garden teems with early-blooming forsythia and redbuds surrounding a grassy glade.* INSET, LEFT: *Chauncey Beadle, shown in 1949 among his beloved azaleas, was hired in 1890 because Olmsted was impressed with the young horticulturist's "encyclopedic knowledge of plants." He said that he came to Biltmore for a month and stayed a lifetime.*

DEERPARK Covering 250 acres to the south and west of Biltmore House is the wooded Deerpark. Scenic game preserves like this were a traditional part of English country estates and were often used for hunting. The naturalistic design—composed of broadly rolling meadows layered with groves of poplar, beech, oak, and hickory—was inspired by the "pastoral" landscape style that developed in the 1700s.

BASS POND AND LAGOON Water features were an important aspect of the pastoral landscape, and Olmsted planned two for the Estate. The Bass Pond, created from an old creek-fed millpond, is just south of the Azalea Garden. Guests out for a walk at the "end" of the gardens could rest at the boathouse or take in the view from a footbridge spanning a waterfall that spills into a rocky ravine. In addition to its beauty, the Pond is remarkable for an engineering feat: Olmsted installed a flume system for flood control that pipes debris-filled storm water under the lake bed.

The placid Lagoon is located on the lower drive and acts as a mirror for the maple, sweet gum, and river birch lining its shore and for the western facade of the House. Like the Bass Pond, the Lagoon was used for recreation.

LEFT: *The tranquil Lagoon was used by guests for fishing and rowing.* ABOVE: *The rustic boathouse overlooking the Bass Pond offers a peaceful resting place after a garden stroll; Olmsted incorporated similar structures into his designs for many public parks.* INSET, BELOW: *In autumn the hardwoods in the Deerpark put on a splendid foliage display. Olmsted created such serene pastoral settings to have a soothing effect on the spirit.*

FOREST The rich woodlands that blanket much of the Estate hold an important place in the history of American forestry and conservation. Although the trees seem to be virgin stands, many were in fact planted as part of a comprehensive land management program initiated by Olmsted and developed by Gifford Pinchot, the first practicing professional forester in America.

The native woodlands at Biltmore had been badly degraded through overfarming, overcutting, and burning before Mr. Vanderbilt acquired the property—so much so that Olmsted advised him against installing an extensive park like those he had admired in Europe. Instead, proposed the designer, the site could be turned into productive timberland that would not only contribute to the Estate but also serve the country as the first organized attempt at forestry. Olmsted enlisted Pinchot in 1891 to rehabilitate the woodland. The land use plan the young forester devised, which involved identifying tree varieties, improving growth of desirable species by selective thinning, and planting for maximum timber yield, was the first of its kind in the country and served as a national model.

When Pinchot left Biltmore in 1895 to establish what would become the U.S. Forest

Service, his work was continued by Dr. Carl Schenck (1868–1955), a prominent German forester invited to America by Mr. Vanderbilt. In addition to installing several new experimental plantations of indigenous species, including Eastern white pine, oak, walnut, cherry, and beech, Schenck founded the Biltmore Forest School in 1898 to train enough workers for the 100,000-acre timberland. The school operated until 1913, educating the first generation of American foresters in conservation techniques that remain influential today.

There are now about 4,500 acres of forest land at Biltmore. Selective thinning, pruning, and harvesting of mature trees remain essential to current forest management, with timber sales providing some of the financial support for Estate operations. Recently revised, a new management plan is in place, designed to improve the quality not only of the woodlands, but also of the soil, water, and wildlife habitats and to preserve the forest in harmony with Olmsted's historic landscape.

OPPOSITE: *Much of Biltmore's lush woodland, the first forest in the country to be managed scientifically, was planted in the 1890s; today it covers some 4,500 acres.* ABOVE: *Stacks of cut timber, shown in the late 1890s, indicate that lumber harvesting has been part of the forest management at Biltmore from the beginning.* LEFT: *Forester Gifford Pinchot (left) was photographed on the Estate with Mr. Vanderbilt (second from right) and guests around 1895; he went on to found the Yale University School of Forestry and the U.S. Forest Service.*

Biltmore Estate Winery

Opened in 1985, Biltmore Estate Winery is a fitting addition to Mr. Vanderbilt's vision. The enterprise not only recalls the historic estate wineries of Europe but also reaffirms the century-old Biltmore tradition of self-sufficiency. Although one of the "youngest" wineries in America, it has become the most visited and among the most acclaimed, having earned more than 100 awards in its first decade.

*J*UST AS BILTMORE HOUSE PRESERVES THE ARCHItectural heritage of the Estate, the Winery perpetuates its agricultural legacy. Rich farmland that once supported produce crops has been given over to vineyards, and the former dairy complex now houses the extensive wine-making operation. The Winery also carries on Mr. Vanderbilt's interest in technology and insistence on quality: state-of-the-art equipment is used at every step in producing Biltmore's premier wines.

WINERY The Winery is located in a building designed by Richard Morris Hunt for Biltmore's dairy, which began in 1896 as part of a large farm operation that also included produce and livestock. Like Biltmore House, the dairy barn was thoroughly modern—from the ice-cooled pipeline that delivered milk into a creamery that once stood across the street to the underground rail system that hauled away used stall bedding. The dairy became one of the Estate's most successful enterprises: its eggs, milk, butter, and cheese were sold throughout Asheville and the Southeast, and ice cream was served at a dairy bar next to this main building.

The facility was occupied by the dairy until 1958 and was reopened as the Winery in 1985 after a three-year renovation. Covering 90,000 square feet, the handsome pebbledash building proved remarkably adaptable in being converted to a new use. The old haymow became visitors' areas, and the three wings of the barn, where more than 200 cows had been housed, were turned into tasting and bottling rooms. The structural vaults in the basement, which have a constant temperature of 54 degrees—the perfect temperature for a wine cellar—were an ideal place to keep wines and sparkling wines during aging.

OPPOSITE: *After a three-year renovation, the former dairy became the Winery. Its central clock tower, with a "candle-snuffer" roof, originally had only three working clock faces; the side toward the pasture featured a painted-on clock, as the grazing cows did not need to know the time.*
ABOVE: *Biltmore Dairy Farms milkmen, seen here around 1930, delivered milk, cheese, butter, and eggs in their fleet of dry-ice-cooled trucks.* LEFT: *An aerial photograph from the 1920s shows the unusual design of the dairy barn, with its three long wings. Today these have been converted to house the Winery's Tasting and Bottling Rooms.*

VINEYARDS Biltmore began experimenting with wine making in the 1970s. The first vines were planted in 1971, in a plot near the Conservatory greenhouses, and the first wines produced six years later (it generally takes four to eight years for vines to mature enough to yield a full crop). The regional climate—with its warm days, cool nights, and mild winter temperatures—is quite hospitable to grapes; in fact, wine has been made in North Carolina as far back as the colonial era.

While the vineyards were initially planted with indigenous grapes, then with French-

American hybrids, they have now been given over to *Vitis vinifera*—the European grape species from which all world-class wines are produced. Some 58,000 vines thrive on about 80 gently sloping acres in the western portion of the Estate, constituting one of the largest plantings of vinifera grapes east of the Mississippi River. A lake was constructed on the site to insure a favorable microclimate: the water creates a little pocket of warmth beside the vineyards, helping combat the late spring frosts that threaten young buds.

Among the grape varieties under cultivation are Cabernet Sauvignon, Cabernet Franc, and Merlot, which yield red wines, along with Chardonnay and Riesling, which are used in making white wines. Chardonnay grapes also go into the sparkling wine.

Each year between August and October, Biltmore's employees gather in the vineyards to pick grapes under the supervision of Bernard Delille, a classically trained wine master from France. The clusters are painstakingly picked by hand to insure that only ripe, perfect "berries" are selected. With a harvest of about 200 tons of grapes annually, the vineyards satisfy almost half the Winery's production capacity.

ABOVE: *At harvest time clusters of grapes are picked by hand under the direction of Biltmore's French wine master.* RIGHT: *Covering about 80 acres along the banks of a lake, which was specially created to aid plant growth, the vineyards produce some 200 tons of grapes each year.*

WINE PRODUCTION Wine making at Biltmore is a combination of state-of-the-art technology and Old World technique. Although the Winery is one of the leading researchers in viticulture in the East and uses the most advanced equipment, it follows centuries-old practices developed in Europe to produce the finest wines. As a result, its wines have earned a remarkable number of awards—including gold and double-gold medals in prestigious national and international competitions.

The Winery produces 45,000 cases of wine each year in about 15 varieties. The production process begins when the "must," or crushed grapes, is piped into a series of stainless-steel fermentation tanks, with capacities between 3,000 and 5,000 gallons, in the Fermentation Room. Grapes for red wine are processed with their skins for flavor and color in computer-controlled rotating tanks for 8 to 21 days, whereas grapes for white wine are fermented without their skins in vertical tanks for up to a month. During fermentation the sugar in the grapes converts to alcohol; when all the sugar is "fermented out," the wine is dry.

The next step is aging, which develops the wine's flavor and bouquet. Because the grapes differ from year to year depending on weather and rainfall, the wine master must determine the proper treatment and aging time for each vintage. Generally, the white wines are aged briefly in the stainless-steel tanks and the red wines are aged for one to two years in oak casks in the Barrel Room.

The aged wines are bottled in an atmosphere-controlled "clean" room, where the air is filtered and exchanged about every 60 seconds—indicative of the Winery's high standards for purity. Running along an automated assembly line, sterilized bottles are filled, corked, capped, and labeled at a rate of 50 per minute.

Sparkling wines are bottled by hand, a process that visitors can view several times each year. These wines are made by the *méthode champenoise*—the method used for French champagne—which calls for a second fermentation in the bottle to produce the distinctive sparkle. At the end of that two-year process, the bottles are stored neck down on special racks and turned daily. This technique, known as riddling, traps sediment, which is then frozen and disgorged; to replace this "lost" liquid, the bottles are topped with a *dosage*, a special mixture of wine and sugar, before being corked. Riddling racks are on display in the Cellars, where wines and wine barrels are stored in the stone alcoves.

OPPOSITE: *Two white wines— Chardonnay and Sauvignon Blanc—and all the red wines age in casks made of French or American oak; tannin and other natural substances in the wood, which is lightly charred, enhance the wine's flavor.*
ABOVE: *Chateau Biltmore Chardonnay, which is produced exclusively from grapes grown on the Estate, is one of the more than 100 Biltmore wines that have won awards.*
LEFT: *Sparkling wines, which must ferment in the bottle for two years in a cool, dark place, are stored in the Cellars. After fermentation is complete, the bottles are placed at an inverted angle on a riddling rack.*

BELOW: *Known for their record-breaking milk production, Biltmore's pedigreed Jersey cows are shown here around 1939 awaiting their turn in the milking parlor. The barn features a clerestory ceiling, which admits natural light, and scissor trusses, a type of flexible roof support that gives with changes in humidity.*
OPPOSITE: *Stenciled designs, including the Vanderbilt family crest (inset, above), create a festive atmosphere in the Tasting Room, where guests can sample Biltmore's wines.*

TASTING ROOM The spacious Tasting Room, with giant scissor trusses crisscrossing beneath the clerestory ceiling, was originally home to 80 cows. In tribute to its former incarnation, the room was stenciled in a pattern called Victorian Barn, created for Biltmore by John Finney, the artist who restored the elaborately stenciled Victorian-era barns of the British royal family. The design also incorporates the Vanderbilt and Cecil family crests.

In this attractive setting guests are invited to sample different wines at their own pace; for novices and connoisseurs alike, part of the pleasure of wine is discovering new varieties that suit their individual palate. Specially trained hosts are always on hand to assist with tasting techniques, discuss the characteristics of different varietals (a "varietal" wine is named for the dominant grape variety from which it is made), and explain how wine can be used to complement food.

The broad range of Biltmore Estate wines—from the light, delicate Chardonnay Sur Lies to the full-bodied Cardinal's Crest—offers numerous possibilities for enhancing a meal. A classic dry white varietal, such as Sauvignon Blanc, for example, is considered particularly good with seafood. A semi-sweet Chardonnay might be recommended to accompany pasta or poultry. Dry red wines, such as Cabernet Sauvignon, bring out the flavor of meat dishes. Sweet rosés make delicious dessert wines—especially with fruits or chocolate—while sparkling wine can be served with all types of food and at any course.

Adjacent to the Tasting Room—on the site of the former ice cream bar—is a large gift shop with wines, wine glasses and other accoutrements, gourmet foods, and cookbooks.

BILTMORE HOUSE IS FILLED WITH THOUSANDS OF OBJECTS THAT Mr. Vanderbilt purchased expressly for his new home—including furniture, works of fine and decorative art, books, textiles, and housewares. Listed here, room by room, is an account of the collection, categorized under furniture, paintings and prints, and decorative objects. As in any residence, housekeeping sometimes requires rearrangement; Biltmore requests the guests' understanding if an object is not found in the room specified.

Biltmore House Collections

ENTRANCE HALL

Furniture
Strong chest, iron, Spanish, 17th c.
Elizabethan-style carved humpback chest, English, 19th c.
Armchair, tooled leather, Spanish, 19th c.
Renaissance-style table, oak, designed by Richard Morris Hunt (1828–95), American, 19th c.
Tall-case clock, Johannes Numan, Amsterdam, ca. 1750
Spanish provincial side chairs and sofa, 18th c.
Octagon table with three legs, 19th c.
Brass-topped table with turned wooden base, 19th c.
Hat rack, late 19th–early 20th c.
Six lamps, wrought iron, American, ca. 1895

Decorative Objects
Bust of R. M. Hunt, marble, by Mary Grant, Scottish, ca. 1895
Roger and Angelique on the Hippogriff and flanking candelabra, bronze, by Antoine-Louis Barye (1796–1875), French, 19th c.

WINTER GARDEN

Furniture
Bamboo and rattan furniture, Perret & Fils et Vibert, Paris, 19th c.

Decorative Objects
Oil lamps, brass, probably Indian, 19th c.
Boy and geese fountain, marble and bronze, by Karl Bitter (1867–1915), American, 1893–95

BILLIARD ROOM

Furniture
Pool and billiard tables, oak, American, 19th c.
Knole-style leather settees and chairs, Morant & Co., London, 19th c.
High-back leather side chairs, Flemish, 19th c.
Trestle table with column supports, French, 19th c.

Octagon table, Italian, 17th c.
Late Renaissance–style cabinet, carved oak, German, 19th c.
Stamped-leather chairs, Portuguese, 17th c.
Bookcase with drawers, 19th c.

Paintings and Prints
Rosita, by Ignacio Zuloaga y Zaboleta (1870–1945), Spanish, 19th c.
Prints, by Sir Edwin Landseer (1802–73), Sir Joshua Reynolds (1723–92), George Stubbs (1724–1806), and Atkinson, English

Decorative Objects
Blue-and-white jugs, Delftware, Dutch, 19th c.
Pewter-lidded steins, Villeroy & Boch, German, 19th c.
Lamp, bronze, 19th c.
Terrier, bronze, by Pierre-Jules Mène (1810–71), Berlin, 19th c.
Walking Tiger and *Walking Lion*, bronze, by A. L. Barye, French, ca. 1865
Tiger, bronze, by A. L. Barye, French, 19th c.
Standing lamps, wrought iron, American, 19th c.
Globe, C. F. Weber Co., Chicago, 19th c.
Firewood holder, wrought and cast iron, 19th c.
Fireplace set, wrought iron and brass, 19th c.
Candlesticks, wood, Biltmore Industries, ca. 1910
Game counter, 19th c.
Pipe stand, 19th c.
Rugs, East Caucasian, Kuba region, 19th c.
Billiard game counter, American, 19th c.

BANQUET HALL

Furniture
Banquet table, oak, designed by R. M. Hunt, American, 19th c.

Throne chairs, oak, designed by R. M. Hunt, carved by K. Bitter, American, 19th c.
64 chairs, Italian, 19th c.

Decorative Objects
Vulcan and Venus tapestries, wool and silk, Flemish, ca. 1546–53
Vessels, brass and copper, Dutch, Spanish, and French, 18th–19th c.
Armor, 15th–19th c.
Rug, Persian, Khurassan region, 19th c.
Rug, Persian, Bidjar region, 19th c.
Wine coolers, brass and copper, 19th c.
Thirteen replicas of colonial American flags, late 19th–early 20th c.
Two replicas of American Revolution–era flags, late 19th–early 20th c.
Biltmore service flag, with blue and gold stars, early 20th c.
Central pennant: replicas of 15th c. European and Asian flags, late 19th–early 20th c.

BREAKFAST ROOM

Furniture
Dining table, American, ca. 1865
Gilt side chairs and daybeds, 19th c.
Trestle table with column supports, 19th c.
Draw table with satyr legs, 19th c.
Table with melon-bulb legs, 19th c.
Display cabinet, brass, American, 19th c.

Paintings
Clockwise from above display cabinet:
William Henry Vanderbilt, by Jared B. Flagg (1820–99), American, ca. 1877
Sophia Johnson Vanderbilt, artist unknown, ca. 1860
Cornelius Vanderbilt as a young man, by Charles Loring Elliot (1812–68), American, ca. 1839
Maria Louisa Kissam Vanderbilt, by George A. Baker (1821–80), ca. 1880
Unknown man, artist unknown, n. d.

Jacob Hand Vanderbilt,
by C. L. Elliot, ca. 1839
Cornelius Vanderbilt, by J. B. Flagg,
ca. 1876
Maria Louisa Kissam Vanderbilt as
a young woman, artist unknown,
ca. 1840

Decorative Objects
Ivory figurines, European, 19th c.
Vanderbilt dinnerware, porcelain,
Minton and Spode, English, early
20th c.
Vanderbilt crystal, Baccarat, French,
and Webb, English, 19th c.
Bird-pattern dessert dishes, Minton,
English, 19th c.
Moonlight lusterware in shell pat-
tern, Wedgwood, English, 19th c.
Japanese-design plates, Royal
Worcester, English, late 19th c.
Pastoral couples, Chelsea mark,
English, 18th c.
Candlesticks, Meissen, German,
18th c.
Three serving pieces, hand-painted
porcelain, 19th c.
Lanterns, Italian, 18th c.
Reproduction flatware, American,
20th c.
Rug, Persian, Joshogan region, 19th c.
Oil lamps, silverplate, Tiffany &
Co., American, ca. 1890
Architectural clock, French,
ca. 1788

SALON
Furniture
Louis XV–style settee and chairs,
French, 19th c.
Pembroke table, English, early
19th c.
Papier-mâché table with mother-of-
pearl inlay and gilding, English,
19th c.
Petit-point screen, French, 19th c.
Louis XV–style double desk, French,
19th c.
Two Sheraton-style ballroom chairs,
English, ca. 1800
Rococo bombé commode with inlay,
Italian, 18th c.
Pembroke table with claw feet,
English, early 19th c.
Napoleon's game table, walnut with
acacia and ebony, English, 19th c.
Gothic-style table, American, 19th c.
Pair of *torchères*, English, 19th c.

Prints
Woodblock prints, by Albrecht
Dürer (1471–1528), German,
16th c.
Portrait prints, by R. Nanteuil,
French, 17th c.

Châteaux prints, by O. de Roche-
brune, French, 19th c.

Decorative Objects
Napoleon's chess set, ivory, Chinese,
19th c.
Bust of Napoleon, marble, 19th c.
Cardinal Richelieu's hangings,
velvet, French, 17th c.
Letter box and candlesticks, faience,
French, 19th c.
Desk set, faience, J. Borrelly, French,
1749
Pair of candlesticks, bronze,
by A. L. Barye, French, 19th c.
Bust of Louis XVII, marble, French,
19th c.
Bust of A. Miner, bronze, by
Constantin Emile Meunier
(1831–1905), Belgian, 19th c.
Bust of stevedore, inscribed
"Anvers," by C. E. Meunier,
Belgian, 19th c.
Bust of unknown woman, bronze,
French, 19th c.
Lamp, American, 19th c.
Bell-top clock, Robert Harlow,
Ashbourne, England, ca. 1780
Pair of tall lamps, 19th c.
Rugs, Persian, Saraband region,
19th c.

WINTER GARDEN CORRIDOR
Furniture
Renaissance-style chest, oak,
American, 19th c.
Torchères, probably Italian, 17th c.
Italian *dantesca*-style chairs, Bilt-
more Furniture Conservation
Shop, 1980

Decorative Objects
Copies of frieze metopes from the
Parthenon, plaster, by Eugene
Arrondelle, French, 19th c.

MUSIC ROOM
Furniture
Baroque-style settee and armchairs,
Italian, 19th c.
Monastery table, style of the 17th c.
Gothic-style credenza, French,
19th c.
Music stand, carved and gilded,
18th c.
Octagon table with lion legs, Italian,
19th c.
Renaissance-style armchairs, Italian,
19th c.
Late Renaissance–style chest-on-
stand, Italian, 19th c.
Late Gothic–style inlaid sideboard,
German, 19th c.

Steinway piano, American, early
20th c.
Carved side chair with upholstered
seat, Spanish, 19th c.
Brass-studded hobnail chest,
Spanish, 16th c.

Prints
Triumphal Arch, by A. Dürer, German,
late 18th–early 19th c. copy

Decorative Objects
Two ritual vessels, Chinese, Chou
Dynasty (1027–256 B.C.)
Apostle figurines and candlesticks,
by Johann Joachim Kändler
(1706–75), Meissen, German,
18th c.
Gilt statues of St. John and St. Peter,
French, 18th c.
Two figures of water gods, bronze,
unsigned, French, 19th c.
Three parrots, bronze, by
A. L. Barye, French, 19th c.
Torchères, wrought iron, American,
19th c.
Floor lamps, wood, Biltmore Furni-
ture Conservation Shop, 1976
Pair of candelabra, iron, 17th c.
Rug, Persian, Khurassan region,
19th c.
Clock, Coward and Company,
English, ca. 1780
Two lamps, bronze, late 19th c.

TAPESTRY GALLERY
Furniture
Semicircular cabinet, Italian, 17th c.
Stool, walnut, Italian, 19th c.
Cabinet-on-stand, ebony with interior
painted scenes, Flemish, 17th c.
Two gateleg tables, probably by Bilt-
more Industries, early 20th c.
Vargueño (desk) and *taquillion*
(base), walnut, Spanish, ca. 1600
Semicircular fold-top table, English,
early 17th c.
Three Gothic-style tables, German,
19th c.
Gothic-style chest with 15th–
16th c. panels, French, 19th c.
Five Gothic-style *dressoirs* (dressers),
French, 19th c.
Two carved tables, Italian, 19th c.
Sofas and club chairs, English,
19th c.
Renaissance-style carved table,
19th c.
Stamped-leather side chairs,
Spanish, 19th c.

Paintings
Edith Dresser Vanderbilt,
by James McNeill Whistler
(1834–1903), American, 1902

*Inlaid and gilded table,
English, 19th century*

Maria Louisa Kissam Vanderbilt,
by John Singer Sargent
(1856–1925), ca. 1888
George Washington Vanderbilt,
by J. S. Sargent, 1895
Edith Dresser Vanderbilt,
by Giovanni Boldini
(1842–1931), Italian, 1911

Decorative Objects
The Triumph of the Seven Virtues
tapestries, Flemish, ca. 1530
Two majolica vases made into lamps,
19th c.
Inverted basket-top bracket clock,
Edmund Card, London, ca. 1675
Bowl with lid, brass and copper,
19th c.
Collection plate, brass, 19th c.
Icon of Madonna and Child,
Russian, ca. 1810
Reproduction family photographs
Figure of cat climbing into kettle,
19th c.
Busts of George Washington and
Benjamin Franklin, bronze, after-
casts by founder F. Barbedienne
after originals by Jean-Antoine
Houdon (1740–1828), French,
19th c.
Stag, bronze, by A. L. Barye, French,
19th c.
Figures of Hercules and Antaeus,
bronze, French, 19th c.
Four Satsuma-style vases, Japanese,
19th c.
Dromedary and dromedary with
rider, bronze, by A. L. Barye,
French, 19th c.
Elephant, bronze, French, 19th c.
Two bronze candelabras, by
A. L. Barye, French, 19th c.
Four floor lamps with turtle
bases, wrought iron, American,
ca. 1895
Pair of candlesticks, bronze, French,
19th c.
Small box, inlaid wood, Syrian,
early 20th c.
Three rugs, Persian, Saraband
region, 19th c.

LIBRARY
Furniture
Settees and chairs, Italian, 19th c.
Carved table, Italian, 19th c.
Slant-front book rack, designed by
R. M. Hunt, American, 19th c.
Jacobean-style bookbinding press,
English, 19th c.
Fire bench, bronze, American,
19th c.
Pair of two-tiered tables, probably
by Biltmore Industries, ca. 1910

Painting
The Chariot of Aurora, by Giovanni
Antonio Pellegrini (1675–1741),
Italian, 18th c.

Decorative Objects
Lectern with crowned eagle, carved
and gilded, German, 18th c.
Globe, Malby's Terrestrial Globe,
Edward Stanford Geographical
Publisher, London, 1899
Pair of incense burners, bronze,
19th c.
Three goldfish bowls, Chinese,
Ming Dynasty (1368–1644)
Oil lamps, blue-and-white porcelain,
Chinese, 19th c.
Bust of George Washington
Vanderbilt, bronze, by M. Grant,
Scottish, 1889
Two urns, porcelain, Naples mark,
19th c.
Two frames with miniature portraits
of Rubens, Van Dyck, Cellini,
Dürer, Carlo Dolci, da Vinci,
Michelangelo, Titian, Raphael,
and Guido Reni, Italian, 19th c.
Document repository, Japanese,
18th c.
Busts of the French historical figures
Cardinal Mazarin, Corneille,
Molière, Montaigne, Cardinal
Richelieu, Colbert, and Racine,
plaster, French, 19th c.
Library magnifying glasses, walnut,
19th c.
Clock with gilded putti and satyrs,
Spanish case, French works,
ca. 1880
Four lamps, brass on marble bases,
American, late 19th c.
Eight-arm candelabra, brass, French,
18th c.
Three library steps with wheels,
19th c.
Pair of three-legged chairs, probably
American, early 20th c.
Desk set, gilt bronze, French,
19th c.
Tapestry, French, 17th c.
Rug, Persian, Joshogan region,
19th c.

STAIRWAY LANDINGS
Tapestry, *Madonna, Child and
Ecclesia*, Flemish, late 15th c.
Bronze bust, by A. C. Belleuse,
French, 19th c.
Busts of Julius Caesar and Augustus
Caesar, marble on marble
pedestals, 19th c.
Louis XV cabinet with pendulum
clock, French case, 18th c.;
Dutch works, ca. 1860

Gothic-style pedestal, probably
French, 19th c.
Cabinet, oak, probably Italian, 19th c.

LOUIS XVI ROOM
Furniture
Bed, kingwood with rosewood inlay
and brass mounts, French, early
20th c.
Louis XVI–style chaise and side
chairs, gilded, French, 19th c.
Louis XVI–style roll-top desk with
brass mounts, French, 19th c.
Pair of Louis XVI–style console
tables, gilded, French, 19th c.
Louis XVI night table, French, 18th c.
Parquetry night table, French,
early 19th c.
Kidney-shaped parquetry table,
rosewood, French, 19th c.
Gilded floor mirror, French, 19th c.

Prints
Prints, school of portraiture includ-
ing the artists Drevet and Muller,
French, 19th c.

Decorative Objects
Desk set, faience, La veuve Perrin,
French, 18th c.
Two decanters, ruby cut glass, 19th c.
Vases made into lamps, French,
19th c.
Cartel clock, Louis Jouard, Paris,
ca. 1750
Letter opener, French, 19th c.
Desk accessory and candlestick,
marble, French, 18th c.
Three-piece mantel garniture,
armorial style, Chinese, 19th c.
Rugs, Aubusson, French, 19th c.

SECOND FLOOR
LIVING HALL
Furniture
Gilded *cassone* (chest), Italian,
19th c.
Coffer chest, painted leather with
brass straps and lock, Italian,
19th c.
Boulle-style desk with pewter and
brass inlay, French, 19th c.
Rococo armchair with ball-and-claw
feet, Spanish, 18th c.
Two Jacobean-style armchairs with
scroll feet, English, 19th c.
Queen Anne–style settee and wing
chair, English, 19th c.
Table with scrolled stretcher, Spanish,
19th c.
Five gilded and painted chairs,
Italian, 18th c.
Barrel-back chair, English, 19th c.
Settee, English, 19th c.
Pedestal table, style of 17th c.

Four gateleg tables, English, 19th c.
Gothic-style chest, English, 19th c.
Gothic-style pedestal, 19th c.
Travel chest with ivory, mother-of-
pearl, brass and enamel inlay,
probably Spanish, 19th c.
Travel chest stand, American, early
20th c.

Paintings
Richard Morris Hunt, by
J. S. Sargent, American, 1895
Frederick Law Olmsted, by
J. S. Sargent, American, 1895
The Waltz, by Anders Zorn
(1860–1920), Swedish, ca. 1890
Going to the Opera—Family Portrait,
by Seymour Guy (1824–75),
American, 1873
Cornelia Vanderbilt Cecil, by Nikol
Schattenstein, Russian, ca. 1920
William Cecil family, by
Stone Roberts (1951–),
American, 1990–91
Genre painting, by W. Verhoeven,
Dutch, 1851

Decorative Objects
Boulle-style desk set, French, 19th c.
Mah-jongg set, Hong Kong, 19th c.
Woman peasant, bronze, by
Valligren, 1893
Statue of Jean-Louis Ernest
Meissonier, bronze, by Gemilo,
French, 19th c.
Satsuma incense burner with
peacock and Satsuma ewer
with dragon, Japanese, 18th c.,
displayed in gilded wall cases,
French, 18th c.
Statue clock with elephant and
Chinese figure, works by Japy
Frères, French, ca. 1870; French
case, ca. 1750
Two blue vases, porcelain, Chinese,
19th c.
Oil lamp made from a vase, 19th c.
Rug, Persian, Ferahan or Mahal
region, 19th c.
Rug, Caucasian, Shirvan region,
19th c.

SECOND FLOOR
CORRIDOR
Furniture
Two inlaid cabinet-on-stands,
Dutch, 19th c.
Two *caqueteuse* chairs, French, in
style of 16th c., 19th c.
Marble-topped bombé commode with
hairy claw feet, Italian, 18th c.
Two inlaid armchairs with rush seats,
German, in style of 17th c.,
19th c.

Gothic-style credenza, American,
19th c.
Two side chairs with stamped-leather
seats and backs, Flemish, 18th c.
Italian *dantesca*-style chair, Biltmore
Furniture Conservation Shop,
1987

Paintings and Prints
Engravings, by the French and
English artists Woollett, Strange,
Mason, Canot, Vivare, and
François, 18th c.
Study of *The Christening*, by Joseph
Villegas, Spanish, 1880

Decorative Objects
Vase with ormolu fittings, Chinese,
18th c.
Curios, daggers, boxes, netsukes,
and tea caddies, Japanese,
18th–19th c.
Bust of Molière, bronze, French,
19th c.
Bust of Demosthenes, marble,
Wedgwood & Bentley, 19th c.
Bust of a woman, terra-cotta,
French, 19th c.
Bust of Diana, bronze, 19th c.

MR. VANDERBILT'S BEDROOM

Furniture
Bed with tester, Portuguese, 17th c.
Settee, chaise, and chairs, probably
designed by R. M. Hunt and
made by Baumgarten & Co.,
N.Y., 19th c.
Dressing table with pier glass
and large table with twist legs,
designed by R. M. Hunt and
made by Baumgarten & Co.,
N.Y., ca. 1894
Small table with twist legs,
style of 17th c., probably
Portuguese, 19th c.
Chest-on-chest, Italian, 19th c.
Two chests with figured handles,
Portuguese, 17th c.
Gilt mirror with crown, Portuguese,
18th c.
Wall stand, Italian, 17th c.
Cabinet with textile, Italian, late
17th–early 18th c.

Prints
Engravings, by the artists Visscher,
Aldegrever, Wierex, and others,
German, Dutch, and Flemish,
16th–17th c.

Decorative Objects
Two candelabra, brass, Italian, 19th c.
Boulle-style desk set, French, 18th c.
Small tower clock, Austrian, ca. 1650
Double hourglass, 19th c.

Two ewers, beaten bronze, Spanish,
19th c.
Urn, wood, East Indian, 19th c.
Hunting dogs with pheasant, bronze,
signed "P. J. Mène 1847"
Eagle holding a heron, bronze,
by A. L. Barye, French, 19th c.
Figure of Mercury, bronze, inscribed
"AD," 19th c.
Figure of Spartacus, bronze, inscribed
"Foyetier 1832," French, 19th c.
Candelabra with coat of arms,
Danish, 19th c.
Friezes, busts, and urns, plaster,
by E. Arrondelle, French, 19th c.
Picture frame with cover, brass,
Tiffany & Co., American, late
19th c.
Pair of candelabra, brass, possibly
Indian, 19th c.
Rug, Turkoman, Tekke tribe, 19th c.
Rug, Turkoman, Ersari tribe, 19th c.
Rug, Persian, Hamadan region,
19th c.

OAK SITTING ROOM

Furniture
Cabinet-on-stand, carved ebony,
Antwerp, 17th c.
Ebonized wardrobe with painted
panels, German, style of 17th c.,
19th c.
Cupboard, oak, German, style
of 16th c.
Inlaid kneehole desk, Spanish, 18th c.
Two chests, inlaid landscapes,
Italian, 15th c.
Draw-leaf table, English, style
of 17th c.
Renaissance-style table, walnut,
19th c.
Display cabinet, ebony and ivory,
American, 19th c.
Carved side chairs with upholstered
seats, 19th c.
Draw-leaf table, probably designed
by R. M. Hunt, American,
ca. 1895

Paintings
Mrs. Benjamin Kissam,
by J. S. Sargent, ca. 1900
Virginia Purdy Bacon,
by J. S. Sargent, 1896

Decorative Objects
Goddess of Mercy, porcelain,
Chinese, 18th c.; stand,
Biltmore Furniture Conservation
Shop, 1992
Two candelabra, bronze, by August
Nicholas Cain (1821–1904),
French, late 19th c.
Bull, bronze, by P. J. Mène, French,
19th c.

Chess set, American, 19th c.
Blue-and-white garniture set,
French, 19th c.
Clock with bronze figures, French,
ca. 1800
Three ivory-colored vases, Chinese,
18th c.
Urn, Delftware, Dutch, 19th c.
Covered urn, Chinese, 19th c.
Two lacquer figures, Japanese, 19th c.
Four musicians, ceramic, Japanese,
19th c.
Two blue-and-white vases, Chinese,
19th c.
Coffee and tea service, Sèvres,
French, 1888
Upholstered mirrors, 19th c.
Tea set, rose and white, 19th c.
Tiger, bronze, by A. L. Barye,
French, 19th c.
Bull, bronze, by P. J. Mène, French,
19th c.
Man with a glass-blowing pipe,
bronze, by C. E. Meunier,
Belgian, 19th c.
Hammerman and *The Iron Worker*,
bronze, by C. E. Meunier,
Belgian, 19th c.
Pair of candlesticks in form of oil
lamp, bronze, probably French,
19th c.
Pair of blue-and-white candlesticks,
Danish, 19th c.
Rugs, Turkoman, Samarkand
region, 19th c.
Rug, Turkish, Konya region, 19th c.
Rug, Caucasian, Kuba region, 19th c.
Pair of candlesticks, bronze,
American 19th c.

MRS. VANDERBILT'S BEDROOM

Furniture
Bed with canopy, American, 19th c.
Louis XV–style chairs and chaise,
French, 19th c.
Dressing table with mirror, English,
19th c.
Boulle-style table, French, 19th c.
Louis XV slant-top desk, walnut,
French, 19th c.
Two Louis XV commodes with
marble tops, French, 18th c.
Louis XV–style cheval mirror,
French, 19th c.
Two Directoire night tables, French,
19th c.

Prints
Engravings, by Schmidt, Drevet,
Roger, and Wille, 19th c.

Decorative Objects
Figured candlesticks, brass, French,
19th c.

Richard Morris Hunt,
by John Singer Sargent, 1895

Five toilet bottles, silver filigree,
French, 19th c.
Small urn, painted and gilded, German, 19th c.
Two figured candlesticks, porcelain,
Naples, 19th c.
Three urns, majolica, Italian, 19th c.
Desk set, porcelain, French and
Dutch, 18th c.
Elephant, porcelain, English, 19th c.
Rugs, Savonnerie, French, 19th c.
Compote, porcelain, Dresden, 19th c.
Gilded picture frame, 19th c. with
reproduction photographs
Two candelabra, porcelain and
ormolu, French, 18th c.
Louis XV clock, ormolu with
porcelain, by Phillipe Barat,
French, ca. 1760

HALLWAY
Prints, primarily by J. Reynolds,
Nanteuil, and others, French
and English, 18th c.

NORTH TOWER ROOM
Furniture
American Empire tester bed,
mahogany, ca. 1820–40
Six Regency armchairs, painted
wood, English, early 19th c.
Empire Revival chaise longue,
mahogany, English, 19th c.
Pair of octagonal drop-leaf tables,
English, late 19th c.
Console table, English, late 19th c.
Nesting tables, painted wood,
W. B. Moses and Sons,
Washington, D.C., American,
late 19th c.
George III–style bureau, Edwards
& Roberts, London, English,
late 19th c.
Sheraton-style chest of drawers,
satinwood veneer, American,
ca. 1800–20
Fireplace screen, wood and
embossed paper, English, 19th c.

Prints
Nine Muses with Apollo, metal-plate
engraving, by Raphael Urbain
Massard after Jules Romain, 19th c.
Mrs. Musters as Hebe, mezzotint, by
C. H. Hodges after J. Reynolds,
ca. 1795
*The Right Honorable Lady Jane
Halliday*, mezzotint, by Valentine
Green (1739–1813) after
J. Reynolds, 1779
The Infant Hercules, mezzotint,
by William Ward (1766–1826)
after J. Reynolds, ca. 1819

The Snake in the Grass, mezzotint,
by W. Ward after J. Reynolds,
ca. 1803
Lady Anne Stanhope, mezzotint,
by James Watson (1740–90)
after J. Reynolds, ca. 1780
*Elizabeth, Duchess of Manchester with
Viscount Mandeville as Diana and
Cupid*, mezzotint, by J. Watson
after J. Reynolds, ca. 1780

Decorative Objects
Pair of figurines of Dutch boy and girl,
porcelain, German, late 19th c.
Letter opener, ivory and silver,
American, late 19th c.
Desk set, wood, silver, and glass,
French, ca. 1820
Miniature elephant, glass, American, late 19th c.
Miniature screen, gilded brass,
glass, and painted copper,
English, 19th c.
Reproduction photograph of
Lila Vanderbilt (ca. 1863) in
miniature bulldog frame, gilded
metal, American, ca. 1865
Reproduction photograph of
Margaret Louisa Shepard
Scheiffelin and William Jay
Scheiffelin, Jr., ca. 1890
Pair of chestnut urns, painted tin,
probably Welsh, ca. 1800
Bowl on stand, bronze, 19th c.
Picture frame, silver and garnet,
American, late 19th c.
Figure of Pan, bronze, E. Le Quesne,
French, late 19th c.
Andirons, cast iron and brass,
American, ca. 1900
Rug, Turkoman region, Ersari tribe,
late 19th c.
Balloon clock, Marriot, London,
ca. 1800

EARLOM ROOM
Furniture
Sheraton-style tester bed, mahogany,
American, ca. 1800–20
Two armchairs and three side chairs,
Chippendale-style with Gothic
splats, Portuguese or Spanish,
ca. 1840
Center table, French, early 19th c.
Louis XV–style cheval mirror,
French, 19th c.
Wardrobe and bureau, Dutch,
ca. 1755

Prints
Thomas King and Sophia Baddeley,
mezzotint, by Richard Earlom
(1743–1822) after John Zoffany,
ca. 1772

Game Keepers, mezzotint, by Henry
Birche (pseudonym of R. Earlom)
after G. Stubbs and Amos Green,
ca. 1790
Labourers, mezzotint, by H. Birche
after G. Stubbs and A. Green,
ca. 1790
A *Poultry Market*, mezzotint, by
R. Earlom after Frans Snyders,
ca. 1783
A *Flower Piece*, mezzotint, by
R. Earlom after Jan van Huysum,
ca. 1778
A *Fruit Piece*, mezzotint, by R. Earlom after J. van Huysum, ca. 1781
A *Concert of Birds*, mezzotint,
by R. Earlom after Maria de Fiori,
ca. 1778
*Classical Scene with Satyrs, Animals,
and Fowl* and *Abandonment of
Cymo*, mezzotints, by R. Earlom
after Castiglione, ca. 1781

Decorative Objects
Inkwell, bronze, 19th c.
Pair of figurines, bronze, probably
Italian, 19th c.
Reproduction photograph of Lila
Vanderbilt Webb and children,
ca. 1891
Pair of pricket candlesticks, Chinese,
19th c.
Pair of busts, bronze and marble,
French, ca. 1880
Andirons, French, probably 18th c.
Rug, Kurdistan, 19th c.

RAPHAEL ROOM
Furniture
Late Federal bed, mahogany, N.Y.,
American, ca. 1820
Late Regency or William IV–style
chest of drawers, mahogany,
Edwards & Roberts, London,
English, late 19th c.
Late Federal cupboard secretary,
mahogany, American, ca. 1820
Shaving stand, mahogany with
late 20th c. faux-marble top,
English, 19th c.
Regency-style washstand, Cuban
mahogany, Edwards & Roberts,
London, English, late 19th c.
Sofa and footstool, mahogany
veneer with leather upholstery,
American, late 19th c.
Wingback chair, American, early
19th c.
Side table, American, late 19th c.

Prints
The Triumph of Galatea, intaglio engraving, by Joseph C. Richormme
[Richamme?] after Raphael Sanzio
(1483–1520), ca. 1820

*Inlaid armchair, German,
19th century*

Dispute over the Sacrament (La Disputa) and *The Fire in the Borgo*, metal-plate engravings, by Volpato after Raphael, ca. 1780

The Transfiguration, metal-plate engraving, by Raphael Morghen after Raphael, ca. 1800

The Expulsion of Heliodorus, metal-plate engraving, by Petrus Anderloni after Raphael, ca. 1830

Holy Family with Palm (Vierge aux Palmiers), metal-plate engraving, by Martinet after Raphael

The Marriage of the Virgin, metal-plate engraving, by Richard Steing after Raphael

Virgin and Child with Saints Elizabeth and John the Baptist and *The Virgin of the Veil (Vierge au Voile)*, engravings, by Auguste Gaspard Louis Boucher-Desnoyers (1779–1857) after Raphael

St. Cecelia, engraving, by R. Massard after Raphael

The Alba Madonna, metal-plate engraving, after Raphael

La Belle Jardiniere, engraving, probably by A. Boucher-Desnoyers after Raphael

The Madonna of the Chair (Madonna della Seggiola), intaglio engraving, by R. Morghen after Raphael, ca. 1810

Vision of Ezekiel, engraving, by Joseph Longhi after Raphael, ca. 1800

Decorative Objects
Two toilet-bottle covers, leather, French, late 19th c.
Brush and comb set, ivory, American, late 19th c.
Water pitcher and glass, Baccarat, French, ca. 1895
Pair of candlesticks, Parian ware, English, 1850–1900
Reproduction photograph of William K. Vanderbilt, Jr., ca. 1882
Memoirs of John Constable, by C. R. Leslie, London, 1845
Letter opener, ivory, mid- to late 19th c.
Desk set, wood and gilt metal, American, 19th c.
Figure of a cow, Delft, Dutch, 19th c.
Vase clock, porcelain, by Gustav Becker, German, ca. 1880
Pair of wooden candlesticks, probably by Biltmore Industries, American, early 20th c.
Andirons, English, ca. 1800–20
Rug, Turkish, Anatolia, probably Capadoccia, ca. 1875–1900

SOUTH TOWER ROOM
Furniture
Louis XVI–style bed, painted wood, French, late 19th c.
Bed canopy, by Biltmore Furniture Conservation Shop, 1994
Painted desk with replacement top, French, late 19th c.
Commode, French, late 19th c.
George III–style cylinder bureau, satinwood veneer, English, ca. 1910
Chest of drawers with marble top, French, 19th c.
Pembroke table, mahogany, English, ca. 1790
Louis XVI–style center table, French, late 19th c.
Five ballroom chairs with caned seats, Cuban mahogany, English, ca. 1800
Two inlaid side chairs, English, late 19th c.
Two-tiered end table, American, ca. 1900
Sofa, occasional chair, and side chair, Howard and Company, London, English, ca. 1895

Prints
Marie Antoinette de Lorraine d'Autriche, Reine de France, hand-colored engraving, by Roger after Rosslim le Suedois, French, ca. 1790
Louis XVI, hand-colored engraving, by Bervic after Callet, ca. 1790
Louis Alexandre de Bourbon, Comte de Toulouse, Admiral de France and *Claude Louis Hector, Duc de Villars*, mezzotints, by P. Drevet after Hyacinthe Rigaud, ca. 1750

Decorative Objects
Perfume bottle set in railcar-shaped holder, crystal and gilt bronze, Baccarat, French, ca. 1890
Pair of candlesticks, ormolu and porcelain, French, mid-18th c.
Figure group, polychromed biscuit, French, 1850–1900
Louis XIV–style pair of candlesticks, French, 19th c.
Railcar-shaped display case, crystal, Baccarat, French, ca. 1890
Miniature table and two chairs, hand-painted porcelain, French, 19th c.
Pair of figurines, polychromed biscuit, French, ca. 1845
Figure of dove, rose quartz, probably Chinese, 19th c.
Reproduction photograph of four of G. Vanderbilt's nieces, ca. 1882

Andirons, French, probably 18th c.
Rug, Aubusson, French, 19th c.

THIRD FLOOR LIVING HALL
Furniture
Player piano, Wm. Knabe & Co., American, early 20th c.
Three glass-fronted cabinets, oak, American, ca. 1870
Side table, late 19th c.
Three inlaid armchairs with rush seats, German, in style of 17th c., 19th c.
Pair of armchairs with Aubusson upholstery, probably French, 19th c.
Oval inlaid tea table, Biltmore Industries, early 20th c.
Side cabinet with carved and fluted decoration, 17th c.
Pair of carved armchairs with stamped-leather upholstery, Spanish, style of 17th c.
Upholstered stool, 19th c.
Pair of high-back side chairs with stamped-leather upholstery, probably English, 17th c.
Drop-leaf table, 19th c.
Six carved side chairs with upholstered seats, 19th c.
Sofa with two matching upholstered chairs, 19th c.
Two-tiered end table, 19th c.
Table, oak, American, late 19th c.
Inlaid side chair with leather seat, 18th c.
Folding side table, 19th c.
Small table with marble-inset top, 19th c.
Pair of carved Baroque-style armchairs, Italian, 19th c.
Carved stool, Biltmore Industries, ca. 1905

Paintings and Prints
Prints, by J. Whistler, A. Haig, J. Reynolds, G. Kneller, J. J. Hoppner, Van Dyck, and G. Romney
Painting of a William Henry Vanderbilt merchant vessel, artist unknown, late 19th–early 20th c.

Decorative Objects
Set of monkey bandsmen, porcelain, Meissen, German, 19th c.
Stone sculpture, inscribed "Rosset," 19th c.
Hamlet, unglazed porcelain, 19th c.
Bust of a man, porcelain, 19th c.
Stuffed hawk, late 19th–early 20th c.
Pair of blue-and-white candlesticks, porcelain, 19th c.

Blue-and-white standing picture frame, Delftware, Thooft and Labouchere, Dutch, 19th c.
Table ornament-candlestick, marble and brass, 19th c.
Pair of candlesticks, wood, probably Biltmore Industries, ca. 1905
Reproduction Vanderbilt family photographs in 20th c. frames
Pair of garnet wine glasses, late 19th c.
Embroidered linens, with "MLV" monogram (for Maria Louisa Vanderbilt), late 19th c.
Female bust, female nude, boy nude, female bust, miniature bust, and kneeling woman, bronze, French, 19th c.
Turtles, bronze, inscribed with Oriental mark, 19th c.
Covered bowl, 19th c.
Lamp made from vase, 19th c.
Balloon clock, James Robson, London, ca. 1780
Bust of man with book, marble, French, 18th c.
Pair of Oriental vases, unmarked, 19th c.
Pair of Oriental vases with handles, unmarked, 19th c.
Ceramic pail, Oriental, 19th c.
Vase with floral decoration, German, early 20th c.
Pair of candlesticks, bronze, French, 19th c.
Pair of parrots, 19th c.
Multicolored parrot, 19th c.
Footed ceramic jar, Chinese, 19th c.
Opaque glass vase, late 19th c.
Pair of covered vases, porcelain, unmarked, probably English, 19th c.
Pair of candlesticks, wood and brass, 19th c.
Set of three red vases, stoneware, Japanese, 19th c.
Embracing couple, unglazed porcelain, probably French, 19th c.
Pair of vases, porcelain, Royal Worcester for Tiffany & Co., English, late 19th c.
Pair of gentlemen, ivory, 19th c.
Two chargers, probably German, 19th c.
Ginger jar, Chinese, 19th c.
Horse and snake, bronze, by Jean-François-Théodore Gechter (1796–1844), French, 19th c.
Bear attacked by hounds, bronze, by A. L. Barye, French, 19th c.
Lacquerware swords, Japanese
Large container, brass, Japanese, 19th c.

Rug, Caucasian, Gendje region,
19th c.
Rug, Persian, Hamadan region,
19th c.
Rug, Turkoman, Samarkand region,
19th c.
Rug, Turkish, Oushak region,
19th c.
Rug, Caucasian, Karabagh region,
19th c.
Rug, Persian, Mashad region,
19th c.

SHERATON ROOM

Furniture
Bed, painted satinwood, English,
19th c.
Marquetry wardrobe, English,
19th c.
Double writing desk, Edwards &
Roberts, English, 19th c.
Side chair, satinwood, English,
19th c.
Sideboard, mahogany, Edwards &
Roberts, English, 19th c.
Washstand, satinwood with marble
top, English, 19th c.
Side chairs and benches, mahogany,
English, 19th c.
Sofa, mahogany, English, 19th c.
Two nightstands, English, 19th c.

Paintings and Prints
Gentleman, artist unknown, 19th c.
George, Frederick, and Lila
Vanderbilt as children, by
Jacob H. Lazarus (1822–91),
American, 1867
Two young boys, artist unknown,
ca. 1860
Seascape, by M. Becketin, 19th c.
Miniature portrait of Harold S.
Vanderbilt, inscribed "Antoine
Oderica d'après Ch. Chaplin,"
19th c.
Print of William Henry Vanderbilt
and his trotters, Currier & Ives,
American, 19th c.

Decorative Objects
Desk set, porcelain, Meissen, 19th c.
Enamelled compote, Fie Boucheron,
Palais Royal, French, 19th c.
Boudoir clock, English case,
ca. 1800; French works, ca. 1850
Candlesticks, rock crystal and
ormolu, French, 19th c.
Inkwell, brass, French, 19th c.
Two letter openers, ivory, ca. 1900
Lamp, late 19th c.
Reproduction photos of Edith
Vanderbilt, original brass frame
Rug, Persian, Khurassan region,
19th c.

SHERATON-CHIPPENDALE BATHROOM
Marble-topped dresser, 19th c.
Pair of painted chairs, Dutch, 19th c.
Table, 19th c.
Clothes hamper, 19th c.
Pair of pitchers, brass, with "GWV"
monogram, 19th c.

CHIPPENDALE ROOM

Furniture
Chippendale-style tester bed,
mahogany, English, 19th c.
Neoclassical wardrobe, mahogany,
English, 18th c.
Chippendale-style suite of seating
furniture, mahogany, English,
18th–19th c.
Pair of candlestands, mahogany,
English, 19th c.
Night table, mahogany, English,
18th c.
Slant-front desk, mahogany, English,
19th c.
Drop-leaf table, mahogany, English,
19th c.
Magazine stand, painted leather,
19th c.
Side table, English, 19th c.

Paintings
The Young Algerian Girl and Child
with an Orange, by Pierre-
Auguste Renoir (1841–1919),
French, ca. 1881
Sortie du Port-Temps Lumineux, oil
on canvas, by Maxime Maufra
(1861–1918), ca. 1894
View of Harbor in Sunset, oil on
canvas, by M. Maufra, ca. 1900
Two watercolors, by Lady Cecil,
ca. 1920

Decorative Objects
Fire screen, enameled leaded glass
with rosewood frame, American,
ca. 1895
Mahogany bracket timepiece,
Matthew Hill, English, ca. 1790
Pair of candlesticks, brass, French,
18th c.
Four celadon vases, Chinese,
Ch'ing Dynasty, Ch'ien-lung
reign (1736–96)
Pin cushion, Chinese, 19th c.
Two cloisonné covered containers,
Chinese, 19th c.
Pair of stamps, soapstone, probably
Chinese, 19th c.
Ceramic cat on wooden stand,
probably Chinese, 19th c.
Bed warmer, brass and copper,
probably American, 19th c.
Dish, brass, European

Fireplace set, brass, 19th c.
Two lamps, 19th c.
Magazines, early 20th c.
Painted fan, Asian, 19th c.

CHIPPENDALE–OLD ENGLISH BATHROOM
Marble-topped sideboard, English,
19th c.
Two painted chairs, Dutch, 19th c.
Towel rack, 19th c.
Laundry hamper, 19th c.

OLD ENGLISH ROOM

Furniture
Bed, brass, English, 19th c.
Knole-style settee and chairs,
English, 19th c.
Gateleg table, oak, English, 17th c.
Two Jacobean-style chests of
drawers, oak, English, 19th c.
Renaissance-style cupboard, oak,
19th c.
Chest-on-stand, English, 17th c.
Stool, Biltmore Industries,
ca. 1905
Gothic-style cupboard, 19th c.

Paintings and Prints
Lord Burghley, by Marcus Gheeraerts
the Younger (1561–1636),
Flemish, 1589
John Francis Amherst Cecil, by
W. I. Cox (1900–54), ca. 1920
William and Frances Cecil, by
Frederico Zuccaro (1543–1609),
Italian, 1599
Prints of English nobility, by
Fiathorne, 17th c.

Decorative Objects
Bell-top bracket clock, Andrew
Flockart, London, ca. 1820
Stag, bronze, by P. J. Mène, French,
19th c.
Celadon vase, China, Ch'ing
Dynasty, Ch'ien-lung reign
Three steins, burlwood, Dutch,
18th c.
Petit-point fireplace screen,
American, 19th c.
Pair of candelabra, brass, 19th c.
Walking cane, American or English,
late 19th c.
Walking-hunting seat, American,
19th c.
Inlaid box, brass, possibly Persian,
19th c.
Teapot, pewter, French, 18th–
19th c.
Pair of enameled candlesticks,
Italian, 19th c.
Pair of parrots, porcelain on gilt
bronze mounts, 19th c.

HALLOWEEN ROOM
Scale model of Biltmore House,
wood and paint, by R. M. Hunt,
ca. 1890

BOWLING ALLEY
Upholstered sofa and chairs,
English, 19th c.
Two sofa tables, oak, style of 17th c.
Octagon side table, 19th c.
Gateleg table, 19th c.
Dulcitone player piano, Cable
Nelson Piano Co., Chicago
Piano bench, 19th c.
Hand-painted dish, American,
ca. 1900
Table tennis table and equipment,
19th c.
Photogravures of (left to right)
Night and Dawn by Michelangelo,
Venus de Milo, the Sistine Ceiling
by Michelangelo, Nike of Samo-
thrace, St. George by Donatello,
David and Lorenzo de' Medici
by Michelangelo
Plaster casts, 19th c.
Table, 19th c.
Bust of George Washington
Vanderbilt, marble, by M. Grant,
Scottish, ca. 1889

SITTING AREA
Four dantesca chairs, Italian,
19th c.
Gateleg table, 19th c.
Trestle table, 19th c.
Settee, 19th c.
Photogravures
Lamps, English, 19th c.

DRESSING ROOMS
Towel rack, mahogany, 19th c.
Cabinet, oak, 19th c.
Carved side chairs, designed by
R. M. Hunt and made by
Baumgarten & Co., N.Y.,
ca. 1895
Clothing, 19th c.
Bowl and pitcher, porcelain, Minton,
English, 19th c.
Hairbrush
Towels, 19th c. and 20th c.

MAIN DRESSING ROOM
Louis XV-style towel rack, 19th c.
Dressing table, mahogany, English,
19th c.
Sheraton-style pierced-back chairs,
19th c.
Traveling toilet set, 19th c.
Full-length mirror, 19th c.
Glassware, 19th c.
Bottle, 19th c.

Powder jar, 19th c.
Towels, 19th c. and 20th c. ·
Toilet set, porcelain, Minton,
   English, 19th c.

DRESSING ROOM LOUNGE
Carved settee with cane seat, style
   of 17th c., English, 19th c.
Two carved side chairs, style of
   17th c., English, 19th c.
Gateleg table, 19th c
Assorted prints

GYMNASIUM
Parallel bars, exercise machines,
   and Indian clubs, A. G. Spalding
   & Bro., 19th c.
Dumbbells, wood, 19th c.
Floor exercise machine, wood,
   19th c.
Gym scale, Fairbanks, 19th c.
Barbells, late 19th–early 20th c.
Cabinet with various exercise
   equipment, 19th c.
Rowing machine, late 19th–
   early 20th c.
Towels, 20th c.

HOUSEKEEPER'S PANTRY
Work table and stools, walnut, 19th c.
Period food can labels reproduced
   from the collection of Ralph
   and Terry Kovel, Cleveland;
   special thanks to American
   Can Co. for its contribution
   of custom cans
Step stool, 19th c.
Barrel, late 19th–early 20th c.
Oil lamp, 19th c.
Eyeglasses, early 20th c.
Inkwell, early 20th c.
Rug beater, early 20th c.

CANNING PANTRY
Period canning jars
Cold pack canner, Ball, 19th c.
Bottle capper, Farrow & Jackson
   Ltd., London, 19th c.
Cutlery chest, 19th c.
Oil lamps, 19th c. design
Kerosene tanks, The Davis Welding
   & Mfg. Co., Cincinnati
Step stool, 19th c.
"XXth Century" cooler, Cordley
   & Hayes, N.Y.

SERVANTS' BEDROOMS
Six chests of drawers with mirrors,
   chestnut, American, 19th c.
Six bedside tables, chestnut,
   American, 19th c.

Washstands, iron, American, 19th c.
Beds, iron, American, 19th c.
Splint-seat rockers and side chairs,
   American, 19th c.
Toiletry porcelain, Minton, English,
   late 19th c.
Servants' livery, 19th c.
Two chests of drawers, 19th c.
Wardrobe, 19th c.
Various prints
"The Gibson" mandolin, type "A,"
   Gibson Guitar Co., American,
   early 20th c.

PASTRY KITCHEN
Work table, oak, 19th c.
Slat-back splint-seat chairs, 19th c.
Assorted copper molds, 19th c.
Wooden sifters
Cherry pitter, cast iron, "Electric"
   brand
Universal bread maker, Landers,
   Frary & Clark, New Britain,
   Conn., 1904
Scale, brass and iron, American
   Cutlery Co., 19th c.
Bouche iron, 19th c.
Assorted period cooking utensils
Tin molds, early 20th c.
Plates, garnet glass with gold trim,
   19th c.
Ovens, Branhall, Deane & Co., N.Y.
Refrigerator, Lorillard, N.Y

ROTISSERIE KITCHEN
Mortar and pestle, marble, 19th c.
Work table, oak, 19th c.
Sausage stuffer, early 20th c.
Cabinet, 19th c.
Iron tools
Copper pot
Rotisserie, Branhall, Deane
   & Co., N.Y.

MAIN KITCHEN
Copper pots and pans, Branhall,
   Deane & Co., N.Y., 19th c.
Server on wheels, silverplate,
   A. Bertuch, Berlin
Enterprise coffee mill, Philadelphia,
   patent Oct. 21, 1873
Enterprise sausage stuffer,
   Philadelphia
Mortar and pestle, marble, 19th c.
Assorted period knives and choppers
Assorted period food tins
Copper pot, creamer, and sugar
Copper egg coddler
Work tables, oak, 19th c.
Slat-back splint-seat chairs, 19th c.
Brass tray
Copper egg cups and tray
Scale

Ovens
Wooden bowls
Butcher block
Tables
Grinder coal buckets

KITCHEN PANTRY
Tray with place setting, porcelain,
   Minton and Spode, 19th c.
Blue-and-white china, Mercer, early
   20th c.

SERVANTS' DINING ROOM
Marble-top sideboard, rosewood,
   J. & J. W. Meeks, N.Y., 19th c.
Bentwood side chairs, 19th c.
Mission-style sideboard, oak, 19th c.
Dining table, mahogany, 19th c.
Side chair, oak and cane, American,
   19th c.
Brass gong and beater, English, 1896
Oil lamps, 19th c.
Glassware, late 19th–early 20th c.
Prints, early 20th c. and late 20th c.
   reproductions

SERVANTS' SITTING ROOM
Sideboard, oak, Ameri-
   can, 19th c.
Rockers with splint
   seats and
   backs, L. J. Colony,
   Keene, N.H., late 19th–early
   20th c.
Drop-front desk, carved oak,
   Biltmore Industries, ca. 1905
Slat-back rockers with leather seats,
   American, 19th c.
Trestle table, mahogany, American,
   19th c.
Corner bric-a-brac shelf, American,
   19th c.
Three side chairs, oak, American,
   19th c.
Work table, oak, American, 19th c.
Octagon table, mahogany,
   American, 19th c.
Book shelf, ebony, American, 20th c.
Hand-cranked Victrola, RCA model
   VV-IX, American, early 20th c.
Zimmerman autoharp,
   Dolgeville, N.Y.
Folding oval table, American, 19th c.
Cane-seat rocker, 19th c.
Hat rack, early 20th c.
Oil lamp, 19th c.
Checkerboard, ca. 1900
Dogs, early 20th c.
Cats, early 20th c.
Prints, early 20th c. and modern
   reproductions

Wooden ball and tenpins,
Brunswick-Balke-Collender
Company, 19th century

Pipe rack, English, 19th century

Letter box, late 19th c.
Vase, 19th c.
Covered dish, 19th c.
Tablecloth, late 19th–early 20th c.

WALK-IN REFRIGERATORS
Fruit crate labels, late 19th–
  early 20th c.
Milk cans
Special thanks to White Rock
  Bottling Co. for providing
  period Sparkling Water bottles
  for display

SMALL PANTRY
Assorted period cans, boxes,
  and barrels
Special thanks to Nabisco, Morton
  Salt, DelMonte, Wm. Underwood
  Co., and Jerry and Audry Glenn
  for providing items for display

TRUNK ROOM
Traveling trunks, late 19th–
  early 20th c.

WORK ROOM
Vases, baskets, and flower-arranging
  equipment

BROWN LAUNDRY
Washer, The Boss Washing Machine
  Co., Cincinnati, early 20th c.
"Kingston" Anchor brand wringer,
  Lovell Manufacturing Co.,
  Erie, Pa.
"Old Time" wringer, The American
  Wringer Co., patent March 27,
  1888
Two Crown fluting irons, patent
  Nov. 2, 1875
"Heat This" hand fluter, patent 1866
"The Best" hand fluter, H. Foote
  Man., Syracuse, N.Y.
Sadirons
Table-size dampening press
Sleeve boards and washboards
Work table, oak, 19th c.
Slat-back and rush-seat chairs, 19th c.
Pot-bellied stove, late 19th c.

LAUNDRESSES' TOILET
Washstand, late 19th c.
Three cane-seat rockers, 19th c.
Bowl and pitcher, 19th c.
Basket

MAIN LAUNDRY
Simplex mangle, Algonquin, Ill.,
  patent May 30, 1911

Extractor, The American
  Laundry Machinery Co.,
  patent April 28, 1914
Barrel washer, Troy Laundry
  Machinery Co., ca. 1907
Drying racks, Troy Laundry
  Machinery Co., 1895
Work table, oak, 19th c.
Slat-back and splint-seat chairs,
  19th c.
Laundry aids, late 19th–early 20th c.
Bed linens, late 19th–early 20th c.

SMOKING ROOM
Furniture
Metal-base table with petrified-wood
  top, French, 19th c.
Sofas and chairs, English, in style of
  17th c., 19th c.
Pembroke table, carved mahogany,
  19th c.
Slant-front desk, walnut, 19th c.
Carved side chair, 17th c.
Pembroke table with painted
  decoration, Edwards & Roberts,
  English, 19th c.

Decorative Objects
Pipe holder with carved goat heads,
  19th c.
Humidors, brass and pewter,
  19th c.
Round-top clock, French,
  ca. 1850–80
Kovsh dish, Russian, 19th c.
Four jugs, majolica, 19th c.
Inkstand, Delftware, Dutch, 19th c.
Portrait medallions of (on left)
  Queen Charlotte, Duke of
  York, Hamilton, Lavater, and
  Shakespeare; (on right) Empress
  of Russia, Lord Nelson, Herschel,
  Pope, and Captain Cook,
  Wedgwood, English, 18th c.
Elephant, lacquer with ivory figures,
  19th c.
Lamp made from Japanese vase,
  19th c.
Stuffed owl, 19th c.
Rug, Persian, Bidjar region, 19th c.

GUN ROOM
Furniture
Marble-top pedestal table,
  American, 19th c.
Upholstered armchairs, 19th c.
Side chairs, 19th c.
End table, 17th c.
Side table, English, 18th c.

Prints
Engravings by J. Reynolds and James
  Ward (1769–1859), English

Decorative Objects
Fox, bronze, by Joseph-Victor
  Chemin (1825–1901), French,
  19th c.
Lioness, bronze, by A. L. Barye,
  French, 19th c.
Hunting dog and buck and doe,
  bronze, by P. J. Mène, French
  19th c.
Silver trophy, won by Edith
  Vanderbilt for Best Harness Pair,
  American, 1903
Liquor box, burlwood, American,
  19th c.
Basket, early 20th c.
Reproduction photos of Vanderbilt
  family and friends
Box of poker chips and cards,
  19th c.
Box with ivory chips, Tiffany & Co.,
  American, 19th c.
Pair of marble lamps, early 20th c.
Fireplace set, 19th c.
Mounted birds and animals
Poker set, late 19th–early 20th c.
Roulette wheel, 19th c.
Poker chips, mother-of-pearl,
  Tiffany & Co., American, 19th c.
Rug, Caucasian, Karabagh region,
  19th c.
Rug, Persian, Qashgai region, 19th c.
Chamber-top bracket clock, English,
  ca. 1810

BACHELORS' HALLWAY
Furniture
Two Jacobean-style leather
  armchairs, English, 19th c.
Two gateleg tables, American,
  19th c.
Louis XV provincial-style cabinet,
  oak, 19th c.
Renaissance Revival credenza
  and matching stands, walnut,
  19th c.
Coffer chest, mahogany and brass,
  19th c.
Two *dantesca*-style chairs, Biltmore
  Furniture Conservation Shop,
  1987
Armchair, Spanish or Portuguese

Paintings and Prints
Architectural prints, European
  scenes, by A. Haig, Swedish,
  19th c.

Decorative Objects
Victrola, RCA credenza model,
  American, patent 1904
Mounted bear, American, 20th c.
Mounted owl, American, 19th c.

Join the conversation

- Free patterns & projects
- Contests & prizes
- Author interviews & staff picks
- Behind-the-scenes news

www.ctpubblog.com
Creative Collaboration at C&T Publishing, Inc.

Pieced quilts that celebrate American architecture

★ 9 traditional, pieced quilts come in a variety of sizes and color palettes

★ Classic-styled quilts are perfect for building your sewing skills: Begin with simple squares and work your way up to more challenging diamond patterns

★ Full of inspirational photos featuring iconic American homes

American 🏠 **Homestead**

Ellen Murphy

C&T PUBLISHING

11022   US $21.95
ISBN 978-1-60705-807-6

5 2 1 9 5

9 781607 058076

Also available as an eBook